THE
YOTTA
BIBLE

I am dedicating this book to a man who loved me just the way I am. His love for me was so great, that his own son turned his back on him out of jealousy.

My admiration for this man is infinite – he was such a good person, full of wisdom, and so caring and full of love. Not a day goes by that I don't think about him and miss him.

This book is dedicated to my best friend, my soulmate, my one and all, my beloved Opa.

You were a teacher and guided thousands of children through school. May I follow in your footsteps and guide thousands of people through the school of life.

Opa, my angel, this book is for you. I love you!

THE YOTTA BIBLE

FOREWORD

Whoa, is Yotta losing his mind? Calling this book a *Bible*? Really? Maybe he think he's God, now ...

Well, first of all, God didn't write the Bible, people did. And second of all, we are *all* God. We were created in God's image, including the ability to create and make things ourselves. This is my life's work. I created it.

By life's work, I mean all the experiences and knowledge that I have gained and reflected on in my life so far, which I am now giving to you. The good things you could try yourselves, the bad things could be avoided. And when I look back on my life, in all modesty, I have to say there's a hell of a lot that I've got to say. After all, I've hit rock bottom and made it back to the top.

So why *Bible*?

There are four reasons:

1. The Bible is the most widely-read book in the world and has more than earned its place as a model of success and wide-ranging appeal.

2. The Bible is mainly about "Belief" – it's no different in my book.

3. The Bible is about someone who wants to save the world and is very often misunderstood. This is something I can relate to.

4. But the main reason is that I think the title, "Yotta Bible," is great – I really love it – and we should all do what we love!

So as you can see, I don't expect anyone to go down on their knees for me. And anyone who knows me, knows that I would rather die standing, than live down on my knees. When you read this book, you'll notice that I always got back up again, over and over, and I hope you do the same: Get up and live!

Love and enjoy life!

Make the best of it!

I AM NOT HERE TO PLAY GAMES.

I AM HERE TO DOMINATE.

CHAPTER 1

WHO I AM AND WHY I'VE GOT SOMETHING TO SAY

I was at rock bottom. Living in dirt.
On the streets.
Fat. Sad. Broke.
I thought about how to kill myself,
with the least amount of pain,
but guaranteed to work.
I just wanted to die, damn it.
I didn't want to go on.
It was over, I was over, emotionally,
psychologically, physically.

Now I've got it all.
My life is like a dream.
I'm famous, rich, healthy
and happy as a pig in shit.
I make my dreams come true
and enjoy my life in California.

- WHAT HAPPENED?

- WHAT CHANGED THE LOSER TO WINNER?

- WHAT MADE MY SADNESS AND HOPELESSNESS TURN INTO HAPPINESS AND OPTIMISM?

- HOW DID I GO FROM WANTING TO DIE TO LIVING THE LIFE?

- HOW DID I MAKE ALL OF MY DREAMS COME TRUE?

- WHAT DO YOU NEED TO DO TO ACHIEVE ALL OF THIS?

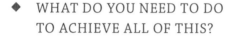

The answers are in this book.

I describe my path to the top, from homeless guy to superstar with his own TV show, from self-hating fat to health and self-love, from the shadows of life to the sunny side of Los Angeles.

My name is Bastian Yotta, and I've got something to say to you! Before we begin, there are a couple of rules on how to read this book.

There are three types of people:

1) LOSERS

Losers are not people who make mistakes, they are people who don't do anything, who don't even try. Imagine a football game. The quarterback is running and running, and keeps on passing, but doesn't make a touchdown. He isn't a loser, it's only a question of time before he's successful, and every time he tries he gets better and gets closer to hitting his target.

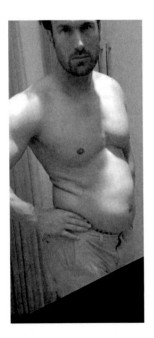

The other guy sits on the field and says: Football is stupid, it's a waste of time, I've never won and anyway my knee hurts. That's the loser!

We laugh at this loser, but unfortunately most people are like him! Many don't do anything – out of fear of making a mistake or not having any success. Every day they find a new excuse or make up a new alibi. That's the loser.

2) WINNERS

He's out there. He keeps trying. He gets better and better. He's bigger than his problems and doesn't make excuses, he finds solutions. He gives his all. Every time. One day he'll be successful - the quicker he learns from his mistakes, the faster it comes. The winner doesn't fail, he discovers what doesn't work and tries another way, until he has reached his goal.

3) PEOPLE, WHO DON'T KNOW, WHAT IT TAKES TO WIN

I would like to, but how? A baby might not be motivated to get up and walk, someone has to show him how to walk. You have chosen me to show you how, and I won't let you down.

Once you've read this book, you will know what you need to reach your goals. So you, therefore, belong to group 1 or group 2. Your actions will make the difference!

I will give you the tools and explain how winning works. What you do with this is your decision.

When I spoke to publishers about my book, I was told I should deliver at least one hundred and fourty pages. I decided I would write a book of quality, not of quantity.

The publishers said I should just add a bit of blabla-bla and a few embellishments here and there.

I said: Auf Wiedersehen, bye-bye, don't call us, we'll call you.

It took a while, but I found the right publisher.

I'll write this book the way I want to, and no one's going to tell me otherwise.

I respect your time. You have a lot going on. Career, family, hobbies. I want to impart my knowledge to you as concisely as possible.

Here goes:

RULE NUMBER 1:

Every sentence has an impact and a meaning. Focus! Skimming through this book won't work. It might be the one sentence that changes your life – don't miss it!

RULE NUMBER 2:

Write down the "aha" moments, make a note in your cell phone. Whether it's a sentence or just one word, you must bring this book to life by bringing it into your life!

RULE NUMBER 3:

Don't believe a word I say. Why should you? You don't know if what I say is wrong or right. All I'm saying is: it worked for me and for hundreds of thousands of students, that I coached personally, or online. Will it work for you? You'll never know if you don't give it a try!

And that's what life is all about. *Trial and error.* Trying is better than studying. But studying and trying is even better!

RULE NUMBER 4:

I write like I talk. With a lot of energy. If you get off on grammar and complicated structures, you're in the wrong place. *Feel* what I'm saying to you. While I'm sitting here, I'm focusing all my energy on my words, which are just coming to you right now. I'm with you, and that's what counts. Feel this book. Feel my energy. We're on this path together!

RULE NUMBER 5:

To hell with my rules. I'm not your father or your teacher telling you what to do. From now on we're going to call the rules *tips*. When you go on a trip, you should listen to someone who has already made the trip. I'll be your navigator. You don't have to listen to me, but if you want to reach your goals, then you should do it.

TIP NUMBER 6:

Stop reading this book. Yeah, you heard me right: stop reading this book right now. Why? Because first I want to know why you are reading. Everything you do in life should have a purpose. So decide what your goal is and why you are reading this book.

Write it here:
I'm reading this book, because

_____

When I've read this book to the end, then

_____

With the knowledge I've gotten from this book I'm going to

_____

TIP NUMBER 7:

Every pilot has a checklist to go through before he flies. Every single time. He knows the list by heart, but he still follows the protocol. I want you to do the same. Read all seven tips each time you begin to read the book. That is your checklist, and I want you to go through it, whether you read the book for five minutes at a time or for five hours.

ALL SEVEN TIPS IN SUMMARY:

1 Focus on each individual sentence, it can change your life.

2 Write down your "aha" moments, so you can remember them later.

3 Let my words follow your actions. Try it out.

4 Be open to what I say and don't just read my book, feel it!

5 Rules are tips, because I want you to be successful.

6 Why are you reading today? What is your goal?

7 Go through these tips before you start to read again, every time.

Great. And now a bit about me, so we can get to know each other better and you'll be able to understand much more in this book. I'm not trying to write a biography. It's about making certain things that I do now and have done in the past more understandable. I want you to understand me because I will be your loyal companion and best friend on the trip you are about to take. I want you to trust me. That's why I'm writing to you about myself.

I am Bastian Yotta. I'm a superhero, who wants to change the world ...

Okay, maybe we should start from the beginning.

I was born in 1976 in Landshut in Bavaria and made it through a brutal childhood. I was definitely not an easy kid because I was always so full of energy, a real little scoundrel right from the start. Today I still have problems accepting rules that I don't understand.

When I understand something, I can give my all. If I don't understand or no one explains it to me, I switch to stubborn pretty fast.

That resulted in regular, massive fights with my father until I was almost sixteen years old. I talked publicly about it for the first time in the TV show *Adam sucht Eva*[1]. My body and my soul still bear the scars. These experiences created a desire in me to one day be free and independent, so that no one can ever hurt me or force me to do something ever again.

Oh yeah, I was born Bastian Gillmeier – how I came to the name Yotta, I'll tell you a bit later.

I was average in school, because I never understood why I had to learn all that crap there. I managed to get my high school diploma with good grades, though. I even learned Latin and Greek because the philosophers of the ancient world always fascinated me.

---

1 The German version of the US TV show *Dating Naked*

When I was finished with school, I began studying business and worked part-time for my father. As an insurance salesman! Let's be honest, kids want to be pilots, secret agents or something like that. Insurance salesman was about the worst job I could imagine. But I wanted to please my father any way I could, and basically worked to win his respect and love.

What I couldn't see at the time was that my father – as far as I'm concerned – didn't love or respect himself and was in that way kind of like a bottomless pit – you could pour in as much love as you could, it was gone immediately. It was a fight that I could never win.

I didn't realize it back then and so I finished my studies and vocational training in only three years with very good grades.

I worked eighteen hours a day and doubled the turnover of my father's business in only two years, which gave my father the opportunity to retire and move to Italy. From then on I ran the entire company and led it to second place in the national rankings.

I thought, I've made it now, my father will be proud of me and finally give me love and respect. I thought wrong! He seemed to always find something to criticize me about. And when things were actually working perfectly, the sucker punch: well, that may seem nice and all, but wait 'til you're as old as I am. Kaboom! What a stupid thing to say. A son can never become as old as his father. He will never catch up, the father is always older, performance can never be measured in the same year of life.

My striving for love and acknowledgment was so great that I even got married early, because he wanted to be a young grandfather. And I love my kids above all else, but they just came too early for us as a married couple – we weren't ready. I write and speak very little about my kids because I want to protect them from the public eye, I'll just say this: I love them no matter whether we have contact or not. I think about my two daughters every day and I am so glad that they are happy!

Then came the day that was bound to come. And it was immediately clear to me back then, that he wanted to bask publicly in my business success and make it seem like the new office and the success of the company was all down to him – I lost my temper.

Could this man not give me the respect and recognition that I had worked so hard for just once in his entire life?

I don't think children should ever have to work so hard for the love of their parents. They have a birthright to be loved the way they are and want to be. That's what family is, otherwise it would be a business, a competition. I couldn't stand it anymore. The work and the relationship to my father was making me sick, so I dropped everything and told him that I was leaving the company.

I wanted to be free. Finally, free of this loveless tyrant! My last words to him were: I just want to be your son – not a business partner, where it's all about money or power.

The last words of my father were the complete opposite.

Even today, more than ten years later, I have the feeling his poor soul is still not at peace. It seems he just can't take the fact that his son is successful and happy without him.

I'm often asked where the mother was who should have protected her son? My mother is to me a loving, but very weak woman, who completely subordinated herself to my father. I think, at some point she simply closed her eyes and didn't want to face who she was married to. He is a master brainwasher, and made me believe, for example, that he only beat me because he loved me. His manipulativeness had the same effect on others. One wanted to believe him. He was always in the first row in church, for God's sake!

I decided I want to be the opposite of my father as a husband. In some ways I'm thankful for everything that I learned from him – for instance, that I know how I don't want to be as a father, husband and person!

DONT MAKE ME
WALK
WHEN I WANT TO
FLY

If I had insisted that my father buy me out, it would have exceeded the entire cash flow of the company and put him in serious trouble. By now I owned almost half the company, on paper. I was very rich, if you looked at it that way.

In order to show my father that it wasn't about the money, I transferred all my shares of the company to him. I gave him millions. An amount that would have given me financial security for the rest of my life. And I did it, because I didn't want to hear one day that I had only gotten where I was through a payout from my father. I also knew that I had paid my father back for everything in a material sense that he had ever given me, such as the cost of my education and a place to live. I wanted to have a clean slate and had paid back more than enough to cover my "debts" with interest. Now, we were even!

NEVER TURN DOWN YOUR **AMBITION** BECAUSE SOMEONE ELSE IS **UNCOMFORTABLE** WITH THE VOLUME

I started over with nothing. I stayed in the insurance business because I wanted to prove that I was better than him. And after he had taken credit for my success a year before (being the second best company in the nation), it was time for a head-on competition.

He started the race with an extremely big company at his back, and I had absolutely nothing other than my know-how and two motivated trainees who came with me. We sat at our desks in the deafening silence. No telephones ringing, no customers coming in. No one knew we were there. All my customers had stayed with my father's business.

My father had basically declared war on me. From bits and pieces that came to me back then, he began talking me down around town, twisting the facts and even putting an advertisement in the paper to mobilize the public against me.

He was successful.

In Landshut, I couldn't even get an ice cream cone served to me. Places where I had formerly felt at home, became hostile. They believed every single word that serious Mr. Gillmeier had to say about his son who'd gone astray.

I kept my mouth shut and pushed everything down, letting it eat me up inside. I knew it was time to push up my sleeves and go from house to house to get new customers. The only thing that could have been worse would have been selling vacuum cleaners door-to-door!

THE
SKY
IS NOT
MY
LIMIT

I should mention that at this time I still had my wife and kids and had a mortgage to pay on a newly built house and other various real estate that I had as investments. All of which stemmed from before my restart.

The pressure was enormous, but I was thirsty for revenge and driven by a burning desire to show this man, my maker, how great I was – and that I was better than he ever was.

What followed was about two years of excessive work. Success was my only priority, everything else came second. I breathed and lived for this one goal.

My team and I ran from house to house and advertised our products. It was definitely a sledge-hammer sales method. We made progress, just not fast enough, unfortunately. I needed to take some time to think because it would take years to get back into the top league at this rate.

I decided to start going after the really big fish. The large corporations with huge turnover. My team and I tried to get appointments with the big bosses, but the receptionists did their job well and kept us out. I decided to go there personally and use all my perseverance and charm. And the critical law of mass took over: my pearly whites and my big balls finally led to success.

I quickly made a name for myself in the business. I was young, highly motivated, willing to give everything and highly qualified. Eighteen hours a day, seven days a week, month after month. I didn't stop to eat or sleep, I was on a mission.

The cash flow was back, the customers were back. *I was back in the game!*

And then came the day of the official rankings. I will never forget this moment. Everything was going great, financially, I was making very good money but that wasn't at all important – I wanted to be better than HIM.

I bought bigger cars, bigger houses, everything to show him: I am the biggest. After all, he had tried to keep me small year after year with the aid of brute physical and psychological force.

As a personal reward for my success I ordered myself a Lamborghini Murciélago and pimped it up to 900 HP. And just as the sports car was being delivered – I actually saw it coming down the street – the email came with the official national ranking.

I heard the sound of the Lambo outside on the street and opened the email in the same second.

Boom! I was Number 2 nationwide, while my father was sunk in the ratings swamp somewhere down around 30+.

I had made it. I had achieved the impossible. I was the only one in the history of the German insurance business to make it up to Number 2 as a newcomer. I had made history and shown my father and everyone else who hadn't believed in me.

Even the aforementioned ice cream parlor in Landshut, where no one had wanted to serve me two years ago, called up and said that I should come over in my Lambo. They had a parking space reserved just for me, right in front of the door. This news made my day because the place was in the same neighborhood as my old man!

But I had paid a high price. I had turned myself into an asshole, that wanted to show off to everyone. I had become a robot with only one word programmed: "success." I was driven by my thirst for revenge and the need to show everyone that I was better.

I had become a machine and the human got left behind. I remember back to this one very decisive moment, as I stood on my penthouse terrace and looked down over my property – I owned a great portion of the street. Seven cars were parked in my courtyard, my beautiful wife played in the garden with my two wonderful daughters, and a question suddenly came to mind. This question would change everything. It hit me like a fist to the face.

I asked myself: *Why the hell am I not happy?*

It was a moment of absolute shock. It came totally without warning and in full force. At the peak of my success I was standing up there crying like a little kid. I realized that I had become a predator. That success at any cost had become the priority. My need for revenge and the desire to prove myself to my father had left little room for any other feelings. I had turned myself off to anything that could have distracted me.

I had won the battle but lost my humanity.

I knew I had to do something.

I had to become human again.

I had to kill the predator in me and start new.

Time for a clean slate – time to hit reset!

I had no idea what to do. But like always in my life, it would be very drastic and dramatic, and that's how it turned out.

However, it was a lot more drastic than I could ever have imagined. What followed were a variety of events that I had brought upon myself in my will to make a change in my life.

First came the separation from my wife and kids. Our marriage by this time had become one of convenience, and I had made a lot of mistakes. I wanted Kristin and the kids to be happy and I knew that I would not be able to help them on the new path I was about to go on.

The universe brought my wife my best friend as partner three weeks after our breakup. It might sound a bit strange, but both of them are still together today, happily married and have two of their own wonderful kids so that my two girls are growing up in a great family.

I remember the conversation with Hansi, when I found out that there was something going on between them. I said to him: If you are serious about her and can make her happy, then you have my blessing. If you hurt her, then I will hunt you down and make you pay!

He promised me that he would be a good partner to her and he has kept his word so far. He's a good man and husband.

Thank you, Hansi!

The separation from my family haunted me for many years in my dreams. I always dreamed that we were happy together and when I woke up I was crying and knew that I had ruined everything.

I still love my ex-wife even today. She's a great person and she was my first real love and will always be in my heart. I'm genuinely happy that she is living the life of her dreams in spite of my failure.

The breakup broke me and today I still don't know whether my heart will ever be able to truly open up to someone new. But more on this later.

With a broken heart, my energy was gone. I felt no motivation to work anymore. I had reached my goal, I had shown everyone I had what it takes. I felt empty and tried to fill this emptiness with material things and squandered my money.

Things happened as they had to. I saw the money disappearing and before everything was gone, I gave the rest to a charity so that it would finally be over.

I was broke. I was a wreck. I had lost everything.

The trip to bankruptcy court felt like the road to crucifixion. Without a doubt, this was the moment my father and his mob of hangers-on from my hometown had longed for.

A shitstorm of hatred rained down on me. Now that I had hit rock bottom, everyone felt free to take a hit at me. All that envy that had built up during the good times suddenly exploded into verbal attacks on me.

I was homeless. My real estate was being auctioned off, financial assets were being held by a bankruptcy lawyer and my self-confidence was level with my bank account.

I was broken and then I hurt my back – it still bothers me today. I wasn't even able to walk upright and that crooked image of me seemed to fit perfectly. At least it couldn't get any worse, I thought. But I was dead wrong!

Suddenly, all I could afford was fast food. All of my accounts had been seized and I didn't have any cash reserves. I slept on the streets since none of my friends were around anymore – after the money was gone they all disappeared. Reality hit me like a punch in the face.

From luxury life to survival mode. Welcome to hell!

One day – I was selling newspapers to survive because when you don't have an address, an MBA and degree in law aren't much help – I saw my reflection in a store window and was horrified: fat, sad and broke – a loser!

It was my daughter's birthday and I wanted to see her. The new family celebrated, but I was an unwelcome guest. They could "never find the time" to arrange for a meeting.

That was the last straw. No one loved me – and I couldn't stand myself anymore.

I sank into a vicious circle of self-pity and anguish. To make matters worse, I lied to the person that I loved the most, my grandpa. He didn't know that I was living on the streets because I didn't want him to worry about his grandson. He would have tried to help me immediately, but I just didn't want to upset him. I felt so bad that I lied to him again during a telephone call and told him that everything was great.

How low can you get? I hated everything and everyone and above all myself.

I wanted to die – just as fast as possible.

Pills? Jump in front of a train? Off a high building?

I had never thought about this before, but now I was seriously considering it.

I thought of all the possible ways to commit suicide.

And the more I thought about it, the more I submerged myself into this one, final mission.

I had totally lost myself. I couldn't think clearly anymore. The pain fogged up my brain.

I decided to jump from a high-rise. After a while, I found one that I thought was high enough to put an end to this disaster. I made it up to the roof after overcoming a few obstacles and sat down on the edge. Only a few inches separated me from a plunge to my death. I didn't look down because I was afraid that I might not be able to jump.

I saw the lights of the city. It was night. I wasn't thinking anymore, it was like I was in a trance. The time had come, I shut my eyes and took a deep breath.

And suddenly I had a thought. A single question.

A question that once again changed my life and prevented my death. What is the perfect life? If a bewitching Jeannie asked me: How would you like your perfect life to be? What would I answer?

Baywatch came to mind. California, sun, hot girls, well-toned bodies, happiness and the joy of life ...

I had to smile at that. I saw myself on the beach, running, I could feel the sand under my toes and saw my chest muscles flexing like David Hasselhoff's. Beautiful babes next to me, the sun shining on my face, and I was happy.

Something had changed. A glimmer of a dream.

I smiled.

It's hard to kill yourself with a smile on your face.

I kept on: I want to be a good person. I want to help others. I don't want to be an asshole anymore. I want to be like a superhero, with all the power and energy of a superhero, but with the right ethical values!

Yes, that's what I want. That would be great!

My heart was pounding.

I was seized by unbelievable energy. I would try again! I would start over again and this time I would do things right!

I looked down into the abyss in front of me and knew, I would make it to the top again but not to jump, this time I wanted to live.

And this is where my story begins.

THERE IS ONLY ONE COMPETITOR:

YOU!

L IVING THE DREAM!

The glimmer of a dream was there. Powerful, yet somehow fragile.

Would this glimmer be enough to generate a blazing fire? Or would it die out as quickly as it had appeared? I had to keep the dream alive just like it had kept me alive!

The dream had definitely saved me from death. No matter how you look at it, it was a really close call.

To everyone out there who feels the same as I did in that moment – here are my words:

It's not worth it. We all have only this one life and we should give everything we have. That's right, dammit. Even when the night seems to be dark forever, it passes. A night only lasts a few hours. There has never been a double-night. Even winter only lasts a couple months. The worst of times will pass.

Don't get sucked into the vortex of negativity. This is exactly what happened to me, and I was inches from death. You have to break out of the vortex, right now, if you feel it.

Because the deeper you go, the more you lose yourself.

Of course, all the regrets you'd expect came to me afterwards: Oh my God, what did I almost do to my children? How my Opa would have suffered! But when you sink that low, you can't think clearly, that's the problem. You lose yourself.

So: break out of the negativity as soon as it tries to force its way in. I see my dark thoughts as an army of enemies. The gate of the mind is open and the first soldier marches in, then the second, then the third. You still have enough power to beat back the enemy of negativity with your positive knights and protect the castle of your life. But the longer the gate is left open and the more soldiers of the devil that get access, the closer they get to taking your village and destroying your castle.

I've been there, I know what I'm talking about. I like the comparison with the knights and castle, because many people know me as King Yotta in Snapchat, and it all begins to make sense. But more on that later.

*

Fair enough. Knights, castle, got it. But what do you do when the first negative thoughts appear?

That is one of the most important realization that I learned in my continual fight against negativity. You ask yourself a question! You ask yourself a question!

This question is the game-changer and immediately closes the gates to your castle. Are you ready? Okay, tattoo this question into your mind's eye and use this tool whenever you need it and I bet it will be every day.

The question is: **What do I want instead?**

This question changes our line of sight in the blink of an eye.

What do I want instead?

What is the opposite of the thing that I fear and don't want at all?

The fear, the worries and my negative thoughts point very clearly to what I don't want at this moment.

Let's be thankful for this info, because all we need to do is pick the opposite of that which we fear and we have our desire.

What do I want instead?

Boooommm! – the gate of the castle is closed. Now it's time to make the infiltrating soldiers of negativity beat a hasty retreat, before they wreak any further disaster.

And it works like this: Stay focused on your crucial game-changer question and embellish your answer.

An example:

You're just about to go on vacation and you feel the flu coming on. The negative soldiers appear on the horizon, coming closer every second, to which you are giving all of your attention in every thought: Shit, I'm not getting sick, am I? Right before my vacation, which I've been looking forward to for so long. Man, that is totally f*****!

Heads up! The gate is open and a couple of soldiers are already attacking your castle, which is a symbol for your vacation, your happiness and your dream life. What's important here is that you recognize that every second counts now!

So ask yourself the question of what you want instead.

◆ I WANT TO BE HEALTHY!

◆ IT'S IMPORTANT TO FORMULATE
  IT IN THE POSITIVE.

◆ YOU MUST THINK:
  I WANT TO BE HEALTHY!

◆ AND NOT:
  I DON'T WANT TO BE SICK.

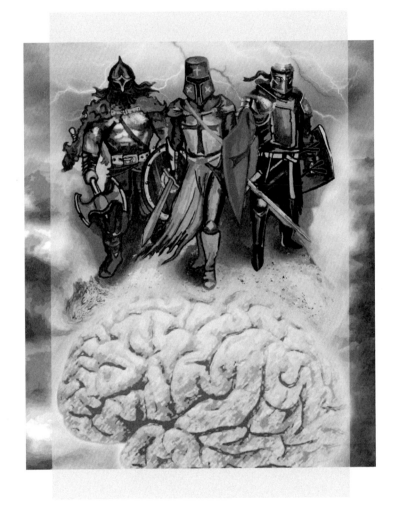

I could now give a long psychological explanation about why that's important. Just say it out loud: I don't want to be sick.

Feel how this statement makes you feel.

Then try this statement: I want to be healthy!

Which feels better? You see, real life is always the best test!

Now stay in this feeling and keep fighting your negative soldiers, because the battle has not been won. You opened the gate, now you have to make sure your castle is "cleaned out" of negative soldiers.

Let's keep the first thought in mind:

You want to be healthy.

Okay, but you probably want more than that, right?

You want to have a wonderful vacation and you want to be healthy enough to enjoy it.

Perfect – half of the soldiers have already been beaten back.

Now we take care of the other half.

Shut your eyes.

See yourself on vacation, see yourself lying on a sandy beach and feel how healthy and happy you are.

Breath in deeply – in and out again. Do you hear the waves? Do you feel the sun on your face and the soft sand under your body?

You're feeling good, healthy and happy.

Very good, my friend! The more you immerse yourself in this picture, the more powerful it works as a weapon against the negative soldiers.

Your fight is showing success.

There are only a handful of soldiers left, then you've made it.

On into the last battle!

Now open your eyes and say loudly and full of power:

I am healthy, I will enjoy this vacation to the fullest, full of happiness and health.

Tada! There's the fanfare. You have defended your castle and beaten back all the negative soldiers. The affirmative knights have reacted quickly again and won the battle!

Congratulations!

And that works the same with everything. You have to understand the system, then you can use it in every situation.

Here's a quick review:

1.   Ask yourself the question:
     What do you want instead?

2.   Embellish the answer, put in as
     many details as possible.

3.   Shut your eyes and feel it!

4.   Open your eyes and make a
     statement: I am ...! I will ...!

Believe me, I did this every day when I was on the street.

Every day I had to build a picture in front of my eyes of what I wanted *instead*.

Your tower watchguards have to be awake every second and be on the lookout for negative soldiers on the march. It is a 24/7 job, you are never completely safe.

But you can now feel calm and protected because you know how you have to react, no matter how many negative soldiers come, this method always works.

I did a lot of work on my thought processes during my darkest times, because my reality was sending me negative soldiers by the second.

I created a dream world for myself and became "pregnant" from my imagination at the time. It is always just a question of time until the baby of positive thoughts is born into the world.

Never, never, ever give up. You are the master of your life and nothing is futile.

*

Some of my readers can probably see their goals but are waiting and waiting and waiting ...

And this exactly is the critical difference. If you are only looking into the future, and only visualizing your dreams in your mind's eye, I promise you that nothing is going to happen. In literally no time at all!

Don't believe me? Read it again.

Just visualizing is too little.

Okay, but what else do I have to do?

Are you ready for the ultimate dream-come-true-tool?

I've already given you a clue: You have to feel the future, you have to feel your dreams.

I call it visuallyfeeling.

That is the game-changer!

Your eyes are invaluable for seeing your goals but when your heart comes into play, now you're in the fast lane!

I always ask my students the question that shot through my head on that fateful night. When the bewitching Jeannie comes and asks you how your dream life would be, what will you say?

In most cases I hear: I want to be rich and happy and healthy.

Well, that's nice, but I didn't get goosebumps when I heard it.

Let's go a step further: Describe the perfect day for me in your perfect life!

I usually get an answer like: I wake up in a beautiful house and have breakfast ...

Cut!

I live in Hollywood – we're going to create a Hollywood movie and you are writing the script. We need some blockbuster ingredients, some emotion and great scenery.

You are the writer, the director and the star rolled into one!

By the way, we are all writing the script of our life, most people foolishly hand over the pen to someone else to write.

In my old life, my father was the director and I was a marionette in search of love and recognition.

How often do we do something just to please someone else or to try to get recognition. How many people are working every day in a job that they don't love! In the USA it is about eighty-five percent. Can you imagine that? Spending a huge part of your day doing something that you don't like!

It's time to start writing your own script. It's your life and you have the right to live the way you want to. But first it is necessary to develop an idea of how your perfect life will be.

I'm telling you: You be the master of your life! Believe in yourself, nothing is futile!

Instead of using the word "master," I like to use the term King, because a King rules his kingdom and isn't there a place in the Lord's Prayer that says: your kingdom come, on earth as it is in heaven?

But it doesn't matter what religion we are born into, we have received the most beautiful gift of all: free will and the power to create. You can create your kingdom and your dream life but you have to be the king or the queen to do this, not the court jester who dances to a different tune.

Clear-cut? I hope so.

It wasn't clear-cut for me for years, and that's exactly why I'm writing this book, so that you can achieve your goals faster and be spared my mistaken path.

Cheers to King Yotta.

Long live the King!

*

Back to the Hollywood movie.

You wake up ...

◆ OKAY, WHAT DO YOU SEE?

◆ WHO'S LYING NEXT TO YOU?
OR ON YOU? OR UNDER YOU?

◆ WHAT KIND OF VIEW DO YOU HAVE?

◆ ARE YOU LISTENING TO MUSIC?

◆ WHAT DO YOU SMELL?

◆ WHAT DO YOU FEEL?

As you can see, a scene in the script of your life is a very complex thing. It doesn't make sense to rush through it like an express train. Everything has to be taken care of just like in a real Hollywood movie, every detail has to be exactly right.

That's what makes a movie a blockbuster. And the film of your life should be a blockbuster and win the Oscar. The Oscar for your lifetime achievement!

I'll show you. Here comes the wake-up scene that I imagined for myself when I was living on the streets and freezing my ass off and had about two euros in my pocket for two small hamburgers at McDonald's.

I shut my eyes and was in my movie: I wake up. Even before I open my eyes I hear the sound of the sea. A fresh ocean breeze tickles my nose and I feel good. I'm warm. I open my eyes and see my girlfriend next to me, she is naked and the sight of her huge breasts makes me suddenly perk up.

Across from our big round bed is a large window and I see the blue sky, palm trees and the sea. My girlfriend opens her eyes and smiles at me full of love and says: good morning, sweetheart, I love you. I give her a passionate kiss.

My housekeeper has already prepared breakfast so that we can start our miracle morning full of energy. I smell fresh toast and hear the sound of the juicer, preparing us healthy orange juice. I smile and I'm totally happy ...

I hope you understand what I'm talking about here.

We need emotions. The word *emotion* comes from Latin and means: move out of. What we want is for our dream to move out of our mind and into reality.

Believe me, it all begins with a thought. That's what's written in the Bible.

Although something got lost in translation. What we know is: "In the beginning was the Word, and the Word became flesh."

Instead of Word, the original text offers *thought* or *reason* as a translation. And I think that is a lot better: In the beginning was the thought, and the thought became reality.

That is the correct translation!

May the churchgoing nerds forgive me for my desire for freedom of creativity, but I have found another mistake. My friends, we don't know, exactly, how it was back then, so I stand up for my right to interpret as I see fit.

Adam and Eve lived in paradise until they were banished.

Cut!

I think the church is making that up because we should feel bad as sinners. We were never banished. We still live in paradise!

Our whole life is a paradise because we can make it ourselves. We have the ability and power to create.

Open your eyes – or better still, close them.

Now, you might think that when I was homeless, I was a long way away from paradise, right? Well, to be precise, I was only a blink of an eye away. Because when I shut my eyes, I was instantly there – in my paradise.

Paradise is inside us.

No one could take that from me then, and no one can take it from you now, because paradise is inside of us.

It doesn't matter where you are right now, it doesn't matter how bad things are going, start creating the movie of your life.

That's how to start. I was once deep in shit, I went through hell and I know what I'm talking about.

Once again, here is a quick summary of how you can write the right script for the movie of your life:

1 Start with the morning of your perfect day: you wake up!

2 What do you see?

3 What do you hear?

4 What do you smell?

5 What do you feel?

6 What are you doing?

7 Who is with you?

8 Where are you exactly? Countryside, house, apartment, vacation, winter, summer?

9 How do you see yourself? How do you look?

The great thing about this movie is you can keep making changes to it.

Believe me. I have woken up with three girls next to me in my movie and we had a lot of fun. You can adjust your movie anytime and create it the way you want.

You are the boss in your world, to which no one has access. It is the world of your own personal fantasy. Isn't that great? What an unbelievable talent we have! Use it and your life will start to change.

Naturally, you can also print out pictures that will support this movie and put them on the wall of your home or your office. The pictures work like a kind of reminder, nothing more, that only works for a few days. Once your eyes have gotten used to the pictures, they stop seeing them.

I prefer fixed rituals, and I call up the movie in my head:

1 The first thing when I wake up in the morning.

2 The last thing before I fall asleep at night.

3 Whenever I need to defend my castle.

4 In traffic or waiting for someone.
Whenever I can!

We tend to concentrate on other people's lives.

Facebook timelines, Snapchat stories, Instagram, news, TV, newspapers – it's always about somebody else's life.

If we devoted this time and attention to our own life, to find out what we really want, and to pull our dreams from our subconscious into our consciousness, the world would look a lot different. *Your* world would look different.

Start to concentrate on your own life because that is the only life that you can change.

When you're dead and standing at the gates of heaven and God asks you: So, how was your life? Do you say: I don't know, but a friend of mine on Facebook ate Sushi yesterday, and Henry posted some pictures from his vacation and did you know that Carl is now ...

You might laugh at my little joke, but friends, that is the reality at the moment! That's what's happening every day. You know more about the life of your friends than you do about your own hopes and dreams!

FOCUS
ON
YOURSELF
AND
FLY.

So cut it out and start concentrating on your own life.

Maybe a reminder on your cell phone would help. Every time you want to see what's happening on social media in the future, put your cell phone down and work on your movie. Or set an alarm so that you are diving into this world at least three times a day to add a few more details.

You can add as many details to your dream movie as you want. The more the better – at some point you're going to become completely immersed and feel the paradise!

You can decide on the color of your bedding or what type of underwear your partner is wearing. Believe me, that is fun. Sometimes I woke up in my dream and my partner was wearing a sexy latex catsuit and instead of saying "I love you" said "Fuck me!"

Your imagination knows no limits. And your imagination is like a muscle, you have to exercise it to make it great. Believe me!

Cut!

Don't just believe me, try it out!

Train your imagination muscles and you will get better and stronger. Every training session ensures the comprehensiveness of your dream and brings it that much closer to reality.

This is the work that really counts. Forget about your job and everything else – the work on yourself will bring you the farthest in the end.

It is so easy you just have to do it.

I personally love to put my script on paper because it helps me to focus.

Here's a quick review:

1. Break out of your old patterns of behavior. Instead of grabbing for your cell phone and checking social media, work on your movie.

2. Set an alarm so that you remember to add more details to your movie two or three times a day.

3. Work on yourself, because that is the work that really matters, everything else is less important.

4. Train your imagination! Unleash the infinite power of your potential to create.

5. You know you are on the right path, when your movie feels as real as if it had already started.

DON'T FIND YOURSELF. CREATE YOURSELF.

CHAPTER 3

B ELIEVE – I WOULD LIKE TO, BUT ...

As you can probably imagine, there were a lot of moments when I began to doubt that I would ever find a way out of my misery.

Man, just imagine: I was the guy with the Lambo and big houses and next thing you know I was on the street trying to sell newspapers just to have something to eat.

That messes with your head, seriously. I asked myself this question over and over again: *What do I want instead?* And I dived into my dream world over and over again, and worked on my own Hollywood movie. But there was always this damn voice in my head saying: *You're a loser! You will never be able to get out of this hole. How can you expect that to work?* My empty belly and the cold running through my body only served to confirm my doubts.

It was a bitter fight. My dream world battling brutal reality. I constantly had the feeling that I couldn't win this war.

How the hell can I believe in my dreams when I'm fighting for my life every day to survive? My dream seemed as far away as Germany is from California – and for anyone who has to swim the distance. That's how I felt: I'm trying to survive in this ocean while my dream is over six thousand miles away. It was impossible.

One day, as I again walked into a department store to warm myself up I went into the book department. I did that pretty often, mainly to distract myself.

I noticed a book from Napoleon Hill: *Think and Grow Rich*. I had heard about the book before. I opened it up and read a sentence that would change my life forever:

"It doesn't matter what you can do, what matters is what you think you can do!"

What!? I was on fire. Something went click, I just didn't yet know what it was. I took the book, sank down into a corner and began to read. The words drew me into their world, hour after hour went by and I was still reading. I read the whole book in one go and devoured every single line, every single word. It was unbelievable, this knowledge that Napoleon Hill was making available to me. I could hardly believe my luck. I had found the way to the greatest treasure!

When I had finished the book I felt enlightened and dumb at the same time. This treasure trove of knowledge had been right under my nose all this time, lying around in the book department, and I had walked by it for weeks, because I was too busy trying to make a few euros to survive.

It was a double-edged sword, because, now, although I had the knowledge of the book in my head, I didn't have a single Cent for dinner – and I was totally starving.

Back out in the cold, I decided to take Napoleon Hill at his word. So, let's see how this new knowledge works in practice, I thought. Having a bit of fun I began saying "money flows to me" while I walked through the streets.

A few minutes later I couldn't believe my eyes and shouted out loud: "Yeah! *I am a money magnet!*" A passerby looked over at me, smiling, and said: "Looks like somebody got lucky today."

Whether luck or visualization, I didn't care at this point. The main thing was, I had money for dinner.

And yet I couldn't sleep the whole night, which wasn't because of the hard ground or the cold, I had gotten used to that. It was the words of Napoleon Hill, that kept going through my head, over and over again.

I decided to go back the next day and read more books on this topic. I was on a mission. I wanted to devour all the knowledge I could.

No sooner said than done. I dived into the material on faith, wealth and the law of attraction. I read a new book every day, sometimes two, I made some notes and studied like a little kid at school.

Now I understood the meaning of the sentence I had so often heard: knowledge is power! When you know that you can achieve anything in life and when you also know how, that is true power!

Just a little reminder: You are holding a powerful key right now in your hands. This is not a book – it's the key to success!

*

Within the next few weeks I had completely changed my mindset and my thought processes and what a surprise – my life began to change as well.

How it worked, I will gladly explain to you.

It's been scientifically proven that when we do something for twenty-one days in a row, it becomes our routine, and our routine forms our character. That's good news for all you assholes out there: You can transform yourself in twenty-one days!

You can recreate yourself at any time. Regardless of who you are or were, you can change anytime.

The most important thing, however, is to change your filter. We take in so much information every second that only two percent of reality makes it into our consciousness, otherwise we would be overwhelmed and collapse. Imagine you hear your own heart beating and the blood rushing through your veins and, and, and ... No, we are built this way so that we can concentrate on what's "important," and what's important is decided by our subconscious filter, that lets in the aforementioned two percent and blocks the other ninety-eight percent.

Do you know what that means? We are actively only perceiving a small fraction of reality. So we had better make sure that it is the right two percent! If you believe the world is bad, the corresponding two percent that confirms this attitude will get through, and you will feel confirmed by this thinking. If you believe that you are a money magnet, the corresponding two percent will get through to you as well, and you will see the world in a different light.

Purely mathematically, there are infinite possibilities of how the two percent can come together from one hundred percent reality. That means that you can create an infinite amount of different realities depending on which filter you use. How crazy is that?

The worst thing, though, is that most people use a filter without even realizing that they are doing it. They aren't taking an active part in life because they don't have any control over their reality.

◆ OUR BELIEF IS ALSO OUR FILTER.

◆ OUR BELIEF DETERMINES
   WHAT WE PERCEIVE.

◆ OUR BELIEF IS OUR REALITY.

And you can take this a step further …

"What you believe helps you!" "What you believe moves mountains!"

Super great, those are some pretty nifty sayings, but how the hell are you supposed to believe something when the voice in your head is screaming that it's impossible and you won't make it?

Let's dive into the psychology of belief. What exactly is *belief*?

This is an easy one. Belief is a thought which is constantly repeated. Whatever you constantly repeat will become your belief. Whether it's a positive thought or a negative one, your unconscious will take it in unfiltered and create your reality from this.

We know this from hypnosis where a person, for example, will think they are a tree trunk, laying between two chairs, and another person can stand on them. Why is that? Because the hypnotist can hypnotize the unconsciousness of a person into believing he really is a tree trunk and it would be possible for someone to stand on him.

BELIEF IS PURE POWER AND ENERGY!

If I'm being honest with myself, then I have to admit I was practicing exactly this kind of negativity for weeks. I thought I was a loser and would never get any further in life. And I found countless examples which confirmed my perceptions every day.

But that's great news because if it can work with negative thoughts then it can work with positive thoughts as well.

And at that moment when I found five euros on the street and shouted out for joy: "I am a money magnet!", I decided that it would be my mantra from then on.

And whenever the evil voices in my head want to tell me I'm a loser, I just reply: I am a money magnet!

The evil voices in my head got louder and louder and tried to convince me: *You are broke and a loser!* But I reacted with more power. With every fiber of my body I shouted: I am a money magnet!

I repeated it over and over again. I shouted it out loud.

This, of course, leads to a lot of laughter when you're homeless and shouting out that you're a money magnet ...

But I didn't care.

Money flows to me and I am a money magnet.

And you know what? The evil voices in my head shut up. Good always wins over evil. You just have to repeat your positive affirmations often enough and with enough power until the evil voices give up!

Wow. I had found the key. I now knew how to convince myself of my new belief. I just had to constantly repeat what I wanted and that is exactly what I did, with all my power, over and over again!

*

The curious thing is that everything changed during these weeks. Everything! I really became a money magnet!

It started when I suddenly started selling more newspapers. Somehow the people were nicer and more willing to buy.

The others on the street noticed and they asked me what my secret was. I began to coach them, for a percentage of their profits, of course, which now began to increase.

I built up my own sales team on the street. I coached my troops in the morning and we all yelled as loud as we could: *I am a money magnet!*

I also trained them in professional sales methods, after all that's what I had practiced to perfection in my "old" life.

I organized team meetings during the day so that my team stayed motivated. In the evenings we met up and thought over together what had worked well and how we could improve ourselves. It didn't take long before this made the rounds and more and more people joined my team. I made a name for myself on the streets.

And instead of two or three euros per day, I was now earning about sixty euros.

My army on the street grew and we became the best sales team nationwide.

My energy and my mindset had changed. I no longer saw myself as broke, I saw myself as someone who had just solved a cash flow problem.

This success motivated me even further and strengthened me along my path.

There is in opposition to the vicious circle a positivity circle. Both spirals function the same, just in different directions. It is your decision which circle you want to enter. It requires a bit of strength and commitment, but it is always possible to switch from a vicious circle to a positivity circle, like I did.

And the right moment for any change will never come.

The right moment is now, right *now*, if you choose it!

One day I had to go to court. Something that should seem negative, but while I was waiting I started to recite my money magnet affirmation. I love the word *affirmation* because its origin is Latin and basically means strengthening. Yes, I want to strengthen the money magnet power.

As I was reciting my affirmations to myself an old friend came along who was a witness in the case, and asked me what I was doing. I said I was in sales and that was true, even if it was street sales.

To cut a long story short: He suggested I switch to the pharmaceutical industry where I would have the chance to sell in pharmacies. I immediately accepted his offer and began training to get the necessary licence. I was finished in record time and began working in the pharmacies.

My life had just moved up to the next level.

What had happened?

After secondary school I had got my MBA with a focus on business law. But my time in the department store when I read all the books on the topic of success, happiness and money was my real degree – from the university of life. I learned how life really functions. And tests in the field confirmed that belief and affirmations are not a spiritual thing, they are a law of life that simply functions.

Period.

This step to the next level was an unbelievable push. It was the ultimate proof that affirmations really work. Of course, I was still far away from my dream goal, but I was a level closer than before!

After only a couple of weeks I was able to afford an apartment and even a rental car. I was back to normal life.

However, I was no longer the same person as before. The arrogant asshole was dead. The streets had made me humble and more human.

Another visualization had become a reality, because that was what I wanted to become – a good person.

In order for you to change your life and get to the next level, here are the individual steps in summary.

1. Believe in yourself and in what you want to be.

2. Create your own affirmations, short and sweet.

3. The affirmations have to feel good when you say them out loud.

4. Formulate the affirmations with all your power and energy.

5. Formulate the affirmations as often as you can, the more the better.

6. If a negative voice is screaming in your head, scream back louder.

7. Create a variety of affirmations, for all the areas of your life.

Today, I am still doing my affirmations, they have become a substantial part of my life. Here is a little excerpt of my all-time favorites:

◆ I AM A MONEY MAGNET!

I actually find money on the street every day and discover countless business opportunities. It doesn't matter whether it's a cent or a million, I am thankful for all the money that I attract.

◆ I AM STRONG, HEALTHY AND FULL OF ENERGY!

Particularly early in the morning, this affirmation is the best breakfast for waking up.

◆ I AM A LOVE MAGNET!

My search for love – this affirmation should definitely not be left out.

And now my absolute favorite of all the affirmations, because this sentence has it all and just feels so good:

- ◆ EVERY DAY, IN EVERY WAY,
  I AM FEELING BETTER AND
  BETTER AND BETTER!

Wow, even just writing these lines I feel unbelievable energy.

You should try it, right now, there isn't a better time to start than right now.

I read this over and over again: *Work hard, play hard!*

We should try this instead: "*Think hard!*" Having the mindset to monitor and keep your positive thinking on track is the real "hard work."

And, incidentally, it's also the most effective!

It requires a lot of discipline to get used to a new routine. People are creatures of habit, and that is exactly what we will take advantage of. We need to set up our routines as positively as possible so that we have nothing to fear from being a creature of habit.

We have created our negative habits over months and years, not least in our language. Expressions such as "not possible," "not my thing," "never" facilitate our negative thinking patterns.

I have shown in this chapter that it is possible to break out of bad habits and patterns of behavior, even in the worst of conditions. You have learned how to do it, now it's up to you to take on what you've learned and change your life for the better.

Do it. Now!

LIFE BEGINS AT THE END OF YOUR COMFORT ZONE

CHAPTER 4

THE PLATEAU – I FEEL PRETTY GOOD RIGHT HERE

The plateau. The deadzone!

Why is it deadly? Because you don't know that you're in the deadzone.

Your life is quite okay. You don't have any reason to complain.

I think most people describe their status quo in much the same way.

If you think like this, you're dead. You aren't living, you're surviving – you're basically just waiting.

But your life could mean so much more. *You call it moment – I call it life!*

Life should be one totally cool moment and not a tedious waiting period for the next weekend or vacation, when you can finally have a bit of fun.

YOU CALL IT **MOMENT** –

I CALL IT

LIFE!

I know what I'm talking about – I was stuck in this rut myself.

After my return from the streets back into society everything was going well. I had a great apartment, another great car, a girlfriend with a beautiful body and on weekends I sat with my friends at *H'ugo's* in Munich and we thought we were God's gift.

And so it went for week upon week, month after month.

In the meantime I had become the Head of Sales and marched myself through the week so I could celebrate on the weekend. Life was good.

But I was treading water. I wasn't making any progress. Not really, I was stuck in the daily grind.

I had defined my goal of going to America someday as a five-year thing. Far enough away so that I didn't have to change anything, but near enough so that it still felt good.

And that was the mistake. It felt good, it felt okay.

Is it okay? Imagine you get married, and you say in the evening about this supposedly most beautiful day of your life: it was okay. I think your partner would look for a divorce immediately.

Okay is for losers!

Life is more than okay. Life should be exorbitantly beautiful.

Back then I liked to use the word "mega" a lot. Everything was mega-cool and mega-beautiful. At some point, however, I came across the metric system and realized that "mega" is not a particularly high value. Mega is about the same in value as a kilo and a kilo is obviously not that much.

I was using the wrong expression every time I had said it!

Or maybe exactly the right one, because my life was just mega back then.

But what was the highest measurement in this metric system?

There it was!

The word that again was going to change my life.

YOTTA.

Yotta is the highest.

That was the day I decided to have a new life, a *Yotta Life*.

I want to reach the highest level possible in life.

It was the birthday of Yotta Life, and I was Mister Yotta or even better:

King Yotta, ready to forge my castle and empire.

I went for a walk with my dog Luna and because it was cold in Bavaria, I froze my ass off. Frost is shit, I hate the cold. How cool would it be to be in the sun right now and be walking around in a T-shirt.

Eureka! Bad weather is a decision, I realized. California has summer temperatures in Winter as well. Yeah, I still had my visualization and my Hollywood movie, but it had somehow lost its power.

I realized that I had slipped into a certain routine. I wasn't living my dream with all my passion and devotion! OMG – I was in the "okay deadzone," on the hamster wheel of daily life. The power that I had possessed to get away from the streets had turned into a routine in which everything was only going well.

My Hollywood movie had lost the emotion. My dream was in danger, the energy was going down and down and it was just a question of time before it would die out completely. It was time to give my dream a shot of adrenaline. But how?

And then I had an idea. I suddenly knew what I had to do – no ifs, ands or buts.

Back from my walk, I sat down on my PC and booked a week's vacation in California, as soon as it was possible. The flight left in three days. It was prime time in the year-end business and my boss would be mad as hell, but I didn't care. The flight was booked and I was a man with a mission. I had to bring back my dream to life! This wasn't about some damn job, this was about my life and my dream!

Three days later I was in Los Angeles. On arrival I felt immediately happy and content. The weather, the city, the people, everything felt wonderful. I sucked in the atmosphere like a sponge. Man, I love this city.

I have to be here! I thought.

And that was the decisive moment. That was the breakthrough. A single word made all the difference again. A word, that all of sudden woke up all my energy for life and made my movie more powerful than for a long time.

Before I had always said: I want to go to Los Angeles!

Now I said: I *must* go to Los Angeles!

I must. No plan B.

"I must" is the precursor to "I will."

And after that comes "I did."

And that is the big, the very big, difference.

An Example:

Jürgen Klopp, the successful European soccer trainer, was once asked which of his players he would nominate for the starting eleven. The ones who would win, right? He answered: No, the ones who *MUST* win!

Do you understand the difference?

We all have dreams and goals, just like I did back then. And I, of course, thought it would be really great if I could live my dream. The moment I stood in Los Angeles, I knew for a fact: I don't just want to come here, I must come here and I will come here!

Every single day of this week of vacation confirmed this even more. I sensed the city with all my being, I fell deeper and deeper in love. My Hollywood movie had not just been brought back to life, it had become my life's blood.

My dream was not an option anymore, it was a MUST.

What had happened? Let me give you a quick summary:

1. Is your life okay, mega or Yotta?

2. Is your dream an option or a must?

3. Break away from the plateau.

4. Awaken your dream to life.
   Give it a shot of adrenaline.

5. Whatever you have to do
   for it, do it NOW!

6. Your dream life has the
   highest priority.

7. No rationalization or excuse should
   be as strong as your dream.

*

Many of us are trapped in a prison that we have created ourselves. We feel obligated to do things that we don't want to do. We think too much about what others think about us and want us to do. We want to fulfill these expectations because we don't want to disappoint anyone, and this all adds up to a giant hamster wheel that we keep spinning around, day after day.

We have friends and an environment that makes us feel comfortable in what we are doing. That's how it was for me in Munich in those days. When I came back full of energy from California and told them about my decision, they weren't happy: Sounds great, BUT ...!

The people around me didn't want me to break away and change – that would have shown them that something like that was possible and they had simply missed their chance.

There they were again, the enemy of my dream. Camouflaged as my best friends and some of them didn't even mean it in a bad way.

IF THEY CAN'T IMAGINE IT
FOR THEMSELVES, THEY CAN'T
IMAGINE IT FOR YOU EITHER.

The doubt your friends have is only a projection of themselves onto you.

You have two possibilities: Either you are very strong and can let everything bounce off you. Or you don't speak to anyone about your goals and dreams. Enemies are waiting everywhere – the evil knights who want to take your castle and prevent you from forging your empire. Ignore them all, because they don't know what they are doing.

I had to be very strong back then, but my dream was too convincing, I had already made my decision. I knew that I had to make a change, to make progress more quickly, because my job back then would never have allowed me to achieve my dream quickly.

And that's what I wanted: to go to the USA as quickly as possible!

I knew something had to happen. I just didn't know what.

And by the way: I hated my job. Pharmacists might be very nice people, but since they have to deal with a new salesman coming through about every five minutes, they can be very rejecting and not always the kind of person you want to deal with every day.

Another very important realization: I wanted to do something that I really liked. I want to love what I do!

Do what you really love and you'll save yourself a lot of time and energy in self-motivation.

The only thing that I knew was where I wanted to go. I just didn't know what path would lead me there. And that's what really counts. We always try to see the path but that isn't necessary. When you have a goal in sight and believe a hundred percent that you will make it, the way will take care of itself – not the other way around.

And that's how it worked for me. I came into contact with the beauty industry through a friend of mine. Such things mostly come out of nowhere and it's easy to say that it was just a coincidence or luck. I always say: the delivery came as ordered.

What gets delivered is what you wish for with all your heart. Or what you fear with all your heart.

Caution: Love and fear are both the same powerful feeling!

Remember how it goes in the Bible: it is done unto you, according to your will!

I would say it like this: it is done unto you, according to your emotional impulse. You are sending out waves at a certain frequency and the universe is delivering accordingly, without any judgement.

Never lose control of your thoughts for this reason, they will trigger feelings that deliver the things that happen to you in your life.

A quick overview:

◆ Do what you love to do, then you are operating on the right frequency.

◆ Control your thoughts, because they influence your feelings.

◆ Your feelings are like a magnet and create the basis for the law of attraction.

Those who understand that, understand life and can begin to take control. Life is your own personal concert, playing just for you. And I'm going to explain how the instruments are played.

You are reading what I have written – that part is the theory.

You have to transform my words into actions, now - that part is the practice.

No one has ever learned to play an instrument just from reading a book about it.

DO IT – that is the key!

Doing is what separates the audience from the player. Do you want to watch how other people live their lives, or do you want to be part of your own live concert?

*

Back to my acquaintance, who told me about this machine for lifting and fat reduction – or better the company that makes the machine. There is a company that specializes in machines that make you more beautiful. That sounds great!

And that felt great, too! I tried one of the test machines and was excited by the results. I invited friends and acquaintances to try it as well and as soon as I had installed it I had a little spa at home, in which our first customers came and went. Word of mouth spread and more and more people wanted to come over to become more beautiful.

My girlfriend at the time was busy almost day and night, the machine worked so well. It was fantastic. I was excited.

I sensed there was more business to be had, but I still didn't want to take the risk and rent a spa in Munich for X-thousand euros. There must be more reasonable opportunities, I thought.

All I needed was a strategically favorable location to reach as many customers as possible for a reasonable price. Almost impossible in a place like Munich, but I could see this room in front of my eyes. I created an affirmation: "The perfect room in the perfect location with many customers will find me!"

I SHOUTED OUT MY AFFIRMATIONS.

I FELT MY DREAM.

I BELIEVED IN IT.

I was enjoying the sun on beautiful spring day and then came the idea.

A tanning studio! There is always a cabin that doesn't work.

I made my way through all the tanning studios in Munich. There it was again, the action after the idea! When I get on fire, I can't hold myself back.

I was in the flow!

I visited the studios without letting them know I was coming and asked for the boss. I asked: What does your worst cabin bring you in profit each month?

He said: Number 7 doesn't make more than two hundred euros a month, the facial machine in there is really old and nobody wants to use it.

I said: In the future Number 7 will make at least three hundred euros a month and you won't have any extra costs.

He was a bit surprised: Really?

I said: I will rent the cabin and do my treatments there and when I bring in new customers, I will recommend you as well. If you send me customers, you will get a percentage on top. Deal?

The idea was brilliant. I got my own place in Munich for three hundred euros in a location where about two hundred customers went in and out every day. I saved a ton of marketing costs because our potential customers were right there under our noses and all we had to do was convince them to use our machines as well.

I did this by offering a guarantee: our customers only had to pay when they had really lost at least a centimeter of fat after the treatment, for example. In this way the customer didn't take any risk – and we had our chance.

It was a Yotta success, and so I opened another minispa in the next tanning salon. I realized very quickly that the concept was perfect. However, I wanted to grow more quickly and didn't want to be constantly polishing door knobs on the search for the next location.

I needed the next big idea.

And it worked according to the same principle.

I SAW IT.

I FELT IT.

I BELIEVED IN IT.

I achieved my goal.

It doesn't matter what your goal is, the system is always the same. Once you have understood, you can use it like a magic wand, over and over again. Time is not a factor. Sometimes it'll be a bit faster and sometimes it'll take a bit longer. You just keep it up over and over again and the delivery will come as ordered.

And that's how it was in my case. I had the idea of a cooperating with a major player to be able to grow more quickly and offer my concept nationwide. As always I asked around until I had found the right contact. I'm like a pitbull, when I bite I don't let go until I've gotten my reward.

After months of tough negotiations and after countless presentations I had found the right one. I got the agreement! That was the breakthrough. I opened two to three locations per week and was on the go and on planes more than in my own bed. Finding employees, training employees, setting up new locations, supervising, making adjustments – I was working eighteen hours a day.

But I was doing what I loved and the success was fantastic. I got up at 4:00 am to get to the airport on time, and got back home at 11:00 pm. This was my normal week. On the weekends I was busy with strategic planning and paperwork in my office.

This only works when these three criteria are fulfilled:

1. You are doing what you really love.

2. You know why you are doing it. You have a goal – and that is your personal "why."

3. You are leading a healthy life and are able to take the pressure – no alcohol, no cigarettes and no other drugs.

I would also like to add that you need a partner that supports you. I have always had that, however the tempo was just to fast for my ex-girlfriends up to now. I am already working on that with a fitting affirmation: I want the right partner!

*

It wasn't long before I could buy the production company. I had then become the manufacturer of the machines that allowed me to work from anywhere in the world.

I HAD MADE IT.

MAKING MY DREAM COME TRUE
WAS NOW WITHIN REACH.

CALIFORNIA, HERE I COME!

This all happened because I had broke out of the hamster wheel and brought my dream back to life again. Basically, my success could be traced back to sixty seconds in which I had made the decision of the century. This one minute in which I booked my flight to California was the crucial minute.

It was the crossroads that went to the right or the left. Right was my dream. Left was my worry: *What will I say to my boss? This is a crazy idea! I can't just leave right now, it's the busiest time of the year!*

I chose my dream. A risk? Of course. But as the saying goes: *No risk, no fun!*

I made the decision to go for my dream and started a landslide. Everything happened in that one single moment. We always say: It takes years to change yourself. Bullshit! It doesn't take years. It happens in a moment. Every change is a decision.

You can fall in love in a moment, you can quit your job in a moment. You can die in a moment and be born in a moment.

It is the moment that can change everything.

It is NOW!

So let's summarize:

1. Focus yourself with all your energy on what you really want.

2. The way will take care of itself – be open with all your senses to all directions.

3. When a door opens, go through it, because you never know how long it will stay open.

4. When the door is closed, kick it in and go through anyway.

5. When there is no door, make one. Nothing can stop you!

6. You must get into a flow, on the wave, because it's like surfing, everything will be simple and easy.

7. Surf on the wave of your life!

I worked eighty hours or more, week after week, and I asked myself whether I should work more, to earn more. At that time, I stumbled across a quote from the Subway chain founder: "Work half as much and earn double as much." It was the moment I realized that to *work smart* is a thousand times better than to *work hard*.

But more about that in the next chapter.

I had broken through my plateau. I was able to move to the USA.

I was ready to begin a new life in a new country.

Doubts? Insecurities?

Of course. But you need to know that the German language and rhetoric is one of my strengths. My liberal arts education comprised nine years of Latin and six years of ancient Greek, however English had never played a big role in my life. I had no idea how to be convincing in English. I had to give up my strongest weapon: my talent in speaking!

You might ask yourself why I wanted to immigrate to the USA? It's simple, it was my dream. So it was necessary to jump in at the deep end.

You always hear people saying: You've got to get out of your comfort zone.

This maxim would mean that I should feel uncomfortable outside of a certain zone.

That might relate to my USA plans, but the spirit of adventure and the need for a challenge were much stronger. I felt motivated!

I basically don't have a comfort zone. The entire universe is my comfort zone. I would only leave my comfort zone if I couldn't pursue my dreams anymore. I was born to make progress and you can only make progress in new terrain. So get the party started!

I didn't want to go to the USA empty-handed.

I wanted to have something in my bag that would make the millions come running.

I had read somewhere that Whatsapp had been sold to Facebook for around eighteen billion euros. At the time the company had had about twenty employees and no big warehouse or production sites. It was something else that made Whatsapp so valuable. Someone had had a brilliant idea and had implemented it.

It was a wake-up call for me. I worked like a crazy person and someone else had simply turned an idea into billions.

And again, like so many times in my life, I asked myself the right question.

A question, that would again have a huge effect on me:

Where, pretty please, is my multi-million dollar idea?

I paused and thought for a while, but no idea came.

No multi-million dollar idea popped into my head.

I was, of course, busy the entire day with my work and had no time and energy to think about ideas. I was trapped in a mini-hamster wheel. Again I had fallen into the trap because taking time to think was an investment in my future and I should have always had the time.

Take note:

WE ARE OFTEN SO BUSY IN OUR DAILY LIVES THAT WE DON'T TAKE THE TIME TO THINK AND BE CREATIVE. BUT THESE ARE EXACTLY THE MOMENTS IN WHICH THE ONE, CRUCIAL IDEA IS GOING TO COME. THERE IS NO MORE REWARDING INVESTMENT THAN ALLOWING YOURSELF THE TIME TO FOCUS AND THINK.

Invest time every day in training your creative spirit. Take time to think!

It's not a coincidence that Napoleon Hill called his book *Think and Grow Rich* and not: *Work Hard and Grow Rich*.

All you need is a very good idea and I believed that I could have this idea.

I created the appropriate affirmation.

I strongly believed that the idea would come and decided to force it.

The brilliant idea would come!

I promised myself that I would write down five business ideas a day for the next two hundred days. When I had a thousand ideas the best one would definitely be among them ...

The law of mass! It was definitely worth a try.

It was easier said than done. The first days were easy, I was bubbling with creativity. But after about fifty ideas I really had to rack my brain to go any further. I sometimes racked my brains for two hours at a time. Sometimes it seemed a lost cause but I had promised myself to do it.

Never break a promise to yourself.

You must be able to trust in yourself.

That is the basis of your self-confidence!

WHAT IS SELF-CONFIDENCE?

The ability to trust in yourself. That means, that you should never break a promise to yourself! Never!

When you keep promises to yourself, then you learn that you can rely on yourself.

Want more self-confidence?

1. Start with little promises, such as:
   Only taking the stairs for one week
   and never taking the elevator.

2. Always do what you promised
   yourself without exception.

3. After you have achieved it, stand in front of a
   mirror and say to yourself: I am proud of you!

4. Make a bigger promise to yourself, such as
   two weeks of not eating carbohydrates.

5. If you break this promise, you have to
   start back at point 1, be aware of this.

6. When you have achieved your second
   goal, then set new goals and learn
   continuously to have more confidence
   in yourself. Because you know, that you
   will keep any promise that you make!

7. Don't make a promise where you
   are dependent on others, it should
   always just be you – no excuses!

STAY FOCUSED.

In this way you develop healthy self-confidence, step by step.

Enjoy this wonderful feeling, be proud of yourself, but don't act arrogantly to others.

In difficult situations, it's an indication of what you're made of. New challenges offer you the best chance to grow.

When you are in deep shit, be grateful, now you can show whether you have the strength to get yourself out of it. Many people complain about such situations, instead of seeing it as a chance to become more aware of their strengths.

WHAT IS SELF-AWARENESS?

You find out your strengths when you really need them – and that is usually in challenging life situations. These types of situations make us stronger. I call them a gym for the soul.

And if you are not strong enough or don't feel strong enough, then become that way. Strength comes from within.

An example: How do my muscles grow at the gym? By my simply being active. I move a heavy object and with continual repetition I become stronger and stronger.

It's the same in life. You have to stay active. You have to get through it. And you will get stronger. You have infinite power in you, let it out, finally. It's there! Discover it! Use it!

I have been through so much hell, I know, that I can have confidence in myself and I have become aware of my strengths. For this reason I abound in self-confidence and self-awareness.

I didn't develop all of this during the highs, it was the lows that made me who I am.

Let's summarize:

1. Every low in your life is a chance to grow.

2. Challenges are the gym for your character and your soul.

3. Become aware of your strengths.

4. If you're not strong enough, then become strong in this moment.

Self-confidence and self-awareness are both factors that you alone can influence, and no one else. Please read this statement to yourself again and internalize it because ninety-nine percent of the time, people let their self-confidence and self-awareness be influenced in the extreme by others.

You have now learned how you can become King or Queen and take the scepter in your own hand. Now use this knowledge, because in your kingdom and in your life, you are the ruler and no one else!

*

Back to my thousand ideas. I kept at it and after two hundred days, I now had an unbelievable treasure in my hands. Now the trick was to find the right idea.

There are two ways to get rich:

1. SOLVE ONE PROBLEM
WORTH MILLIONS.

2. SOLVE ONE PROBLEM
FOR MILLIONS.

First, I put a team of advisers together. I'm not talking about a couple of overpaid consultants, here, who would hand me an invoice for a thousand euros and then tell me that I was now out of a thousand euros.

My team was made up of my grandpa, a good friend and three other acquaintances. We worked our way through all the ideas, keeping the above named points in mind.

How can we solve one problem for millions of people?

That criteria was a bit meager, so I'm adding a couple more ingredients of how to get rich:

1. You must love what you do.

2. There has to be the right niche in the market.

3. The project has to fit to our times.

4. Okay, so I already had five criteria:

What did I love? Definitely my grandpa!
What was his problem?
What was my problem?
Was this a problem that millions have?
After four weeks we had found the idea!
Our young generation uses technologies like social media, photo-sharing and all kinds of things in the internet.

Seniors like my grandfather had a huge problem with this and couldn't participate in these technological advances. This generation had been forgotten. While we continue to network with the world and make new friends on Facebook from around the world, our seniors are getting more and more lonely.

This was the idea! It was great! With my new mindset, affirmations and lots and lots of work I had developed a multi-million dollar idea.

I am still working with my team on this project, today, and it is one of my biggest goals to actually implement it and connect all seniors and generations with the help of technology. And I will not stop until I've achieved it. Even though my beloved grandfather did not live to see the success, I can devote all my energy in his name for the good of all seniors and their children and grandchildren. I still have a long way to go, but as so often in my life, I will rise with the challenge and won't give up until I've reached my goal.

I see it. I feel it. I am this challenge.

As you can see, it is possible to be a money magnet and attract the right ideas into your life. But it takes time and energy. It has to be the most important thing in your life, to invest this time and energy. It's exactly this priority that is the best investment.

We are often so distracted by our daily life that we hardly find the time to be creative. As I've already said: *Work smart, not hard* – but more about this in the next chapter.

The journey continues – there is still a lot to learn.

LIVE
A LIFE OF
UNLIMITED
POSSIBILITIES.

Y OTTA LIFE GOES USA MY LIFE OF UNLIMITED POSSIBILITIES

All or nothing, that is my motto. Because one thing had become clear to me: When I go to the USA, I'm not coming back in a few months just because it didn't work out the way I wanted.

I was going to a country that I had only been to twice on vacation and in which I knew no one other than my real estate agent and an advisor that helped me get a Visa.

Three weeks before the move the evil voices got loud again: *You haven't earned this at all! First homeless and now Hollywood? That's not going to work!*

The negative voice was loud and penetrating.

NOT HERE   **NOT NOW**   **NOT YOU**

I had two big enemies to fight that many of you probably know:

1. The feeling that you haven't earned something or are not worth it.

2. Your own past.

I will now devote all my energy to these two points so that you can beat this enemy back as I did and still do today. It should be noted, however, that you can never kill these enemies once and for all. You can only make them beat a hasty retreat, over and over again, because they will always come back to you.

You must be continually aware and ready to recognize and fight them. These two enemies can come out of nowhere and surprise you with their cunning. Evil thoughts, that try to pull us back into the past and want to tell us that we haven't earned something. In the past it is usually dark, and there is definitely no progress there.

My past delivered images to me that immediately reduced my energy level. Images of me sleeping in a garbage bag because it was as cold as hell on the streets. Or of my father, who was again punishing me by raising the stick.

My bankrupt life! My failure!

All these images are negative soldiers, trying to march in the gate of my mind.

And now I was supposed to go to Hollywood? The voices in my head were loud and insistent. *You haven't earned it at all!*

Here was another important question: Do you always have to earn something?

That's something that we learn from our parents, school or job, right?

Consider this: Did you deserve to be born? Were you that much of an obedient semen or such a loving ovum?

Sounds crazy, but, life is given to us!

Having to earn something – that's something people came up with to control other people.

The church has said: Donate a tenth of your money and you have earned your place in heaven.

The boss says: Do this and that and you will have earned a bonus.

And my father's credo always seemed to be: You have to earn my love.

And now get this: Life is a gift!

The universe or dear God above or however you want to call your faith, gives us gifts every day and without asking for anything in return.

It's called love. Unconditional love.

Life loves you.

God loves you.

The universe loves you.
That's the reason why you are alive.
You don't have to earn anything.
Isn't that wonderful? Yeah, it is. *Three cheers to that!*
A quick summary:

1. You don't have to earn anything.

2. Life is a gift.

3. Every day is a gift.

4. Your abilities are gifts.

5. Recognize and use these gifts.

6. Be worth it and make the best out of it.

7. Feel great.

*

I hate it when people say: You deserved it or earned it.

You don't even have to be a good person to get something.

I know the biggest assholes with millions in their bank accounts who also have great wives and are even happy!

A GIFT.

TAKE IT.

But they don't deserve it – so the key must be something else.

If I don't have to earn happiness, what the hell do I have to do then?

Why do some people get so much and others nothing at all?

The answer is:

ASK	BELIEVE	RECEIVE.

The request for something you desire is a lost cause if you think you don't deserve it or think you're not worth it.

Hey man, this is the point where ninety-eight percent of you fail.

This is the one thing that is standing in your way.

You are standing at the buffet of life and only have to take what you want, and then you turn away and say: Um, I just haven't earned it yet.

It makes me want to rip my hair out, and my hair is sacred to me.

Lay claim to what you want!

With the same vehemence that I asked for my USA dream!

Not: I would so like to live in the USA.

Not: I want to live in the USA.

But: I must live in the USA and I will live in the USA. Period!

This is the little and amazing difference. You've baked your great cake, put it in the oven, and nothing happens. You wait and wait and get disappointed. You did everything right, but …

Turn on the heat!

And with heat I mean the power and energy of the "I must" and "I will."

ASK · BELIEVE · RECEIVE.

Again we're talking about belief, and as I've explained pretty comprehensively, affirmations help you to believe in your dreams.

You have to believe with such intensity that your dream already feels real. And this works when you dream in as many details and as often as possible with short affirmations to strengthen them even more.

Everything else is easy. Lay back, relax and wait for the delivery.

That's it.

I can now hear the outcry: Okay, but I still have to *do* something for it! I have to work hard and carry on tirelessly and all that!

ASK ▸ **BELIEVE** ▸ **RECEIVE.**

Do you see hard work written there?

In fact, this is quite a hot topic at the moment that I'm happy to devote some time to. Many people think they have to work hard to earn success. Every day you hear: No pain, no gain!

Hard work is interpreted incorrectly about ninety-nine percent of the time. Hard work is often confused with "working a lot," meaning: lots of overtime.

This is wrong. Completely wrong!

If you are paid by the hour, then you are limiting your potential. Even the best employees can never work more than twenty-four hours a day. You should never work by the hour!

Okay, but how, then?

The best way to be paid is according to the value that you add to something. This "plus" is the value of your work and not the amount of hours that you spend.

Here's an example: In the summer of 2017 we filmed *Adam sucht Eva* on an island. We worked for about four weeks. I was to be the star, but there were a lot of normal, i.e. non-star participants there as well. All of them were on the same island and did about the same thing for the exact same amount of time for four weeks.

There was just one difference: I earned per hour what the others earned per week. Sounds unfair, doesn't it? It isn't though because we were paid according to "value" and not per hour.

My name in the TV show ensured that millions of people tuned in. And when millions of people tune in, the station can sell advertising at a much higher rate than when only a few hundred thousand tune in. Nobody's heard of the average Joe, his name has no influence on the ratings or the station's income. My value for the station was significantly higher.

Of course, I'm not talking about human value, here, I'm talking about the value of a TV show participant for the production.

And now we've arrived at the main point: Whatever you do, you have to create added value, and then you will be paid according to that.

This is your chance to make millions. You must create the right amount of added value or solve a problem worth millions or for millions of people. And in so doing you don't work hard, you work smart, because then you can aim for a substantial income with very little expenditure of time.

I only work a few hours a day, but I work every single moment on my mindset that I always want to have tuned to the right frequency.

If you believe you have to slave away for hours to become successful, then do that. Everything that you believe is right. I want to show you, however, in this chapter, that there is an easier and more effective way, so that you can have enough time for family, hobbies and other passions in addition to your work.

So change your beliefs! You have already learned how.

Life is based on the law of attraction.

| ASK | BELIEVE | RECEIVE. |

A quick summary:

1. You will be paid according to the value that you add to society.

2. The more rare the thing is that you have to offer, the higher the value – that's how the principle of supply and demand works.

3. Work smart, not hard – but do your thinking every single day.

4. *Ask – believe – receive.*

5. The law of attraction is not a belief,
it is a law. Take advantage of it!

6. Recognize that you can have everything
in life without having to "earn" it.

*

Now we have to address the past (in which, unfortunately, more people live than in the present). Isn't that crazy? We are alive today, at exactly this moment, and still there are many of us imprisoned by past events.

If I concentrated on my past, on all the beatings and the scars that life inflicted on me, on life on the streets, on all the mistakes I made, then I would have a very, very low energy level.

That would only lead to me achieving very little or nothing since I would be constantly distracted by negative thoughts and memories. That doesn't make sense and life should make sense!

That's why you should write down my favorite statement:

IF IT HAPPENED MORE
THAN THREE MINUTES AGO,
IT DOESN'T MATTER ANYMORE

It's the past – move on – it's over!

That might sound strange at first, but it makes sense, for example, when you think about driving a car. If you spend the entire time looking in the rearview mirror, you are not concentrating on the way ahead, the place where you actually want to go. It'll definitely make you go the wrong way, or cause an accident.

I look where I'm going and I don't look back.

If I constantly concentrated on where I had been, I would be moving backwards and not forwards.

What should you do with the past, then?

Learn your lessons, then close that chapter and move on.

Every mistake made in the past should initiate a learning process. The first time something goes wrong, it's a mistake and nothing more. You didn't know that you were making a mistake. But the second time is a decision because you know, now, that it is a mistake.

Only morons make the same mistake over and over again because they are too dumb to learn from them.

So I want to expand my favorite statement a bit:

IF IT HAPPENED MORE THAN THREE MINUTES AGO, IT DOESN'T MATTER ANYMORE, BECAUSE I HAVE LEARNED FROM IT AND DIRECT MY SIGHTS FORWARD TO BE BETTER AT IT IN THE FUTURE.

Even if it was an indirect mistake, I also learn the lesson.

Here's an example: Someone broke in and stole fifty thousand dollars. I can't do anything about that, can I? But, it was my fault! I attracted the break-in myself through my own emotions, through my fears, and the universe delivered.

I recognized my mistake after the break-in and changed my thoughts accordingly. I am not perfect, but I carry out pretty intense self-analysis so that I can learn something from every event. That is supposed to be the goal of each day. More on this in "The Meaning of Life" chapter.

*

Back to my move to the USA.

I didn't have to earn the move, I would move because I wanted to.

ASK **BELIEVE** **RECEIVE.**

I once lived on the streets. Who cares? I learned my lesson and now the next level was waiting for me.

IF IT HAPPENED MORE THAN
THREE MINUTES AGO, IT DOESN'T
MATTER ANYMORE.

I had combatted my two enemies.

And then it was finally there, the day of the move! I was unbelievably excited, because I knew that I was beginning a new life and America was waiting for me.

The flight went without a hitch. It felt wonderful to know that I had reached this totally cool, totally huge goal. It was one of the most magical moments in my life, because I had come a very long way. I had fought my way through countless hurdles and never stopped believing that I could make it. I had made a promise to myself on the ledge of that high-rise, as I stood at the crossroads of life and death, and I had kept this promise.

I had promised myself to give my all, and giving my all was enough. I had made it.

Anything is possible. This book and my life are the proof. I am nothing special. I only made a decision and started along my path. And you can do that too!

I wish I could have held a Yotta Bible back then in my hands, like you are doing now. Use this chance!

On the very first day, my girlfriend at the time, Maria, and I were invited to a big party. A contact that I had met on vacation, had invited us to a reception. All dressed up and motivated we arrived at the villa. I was ready to make my entrance in Hollywood.

At the door of this huge mansion in Beverly Hills a security guard greeted us and asked me my name.

"Yotta," I said full of pride.

"Sorry, you're not on the list," was the sobering answer.

"Wait a minute, that has to be a mistake, I'm going to call the host myself," I said and dialled his number.

"Hello?"

"Hello, Yotta here, we're standing outside your front door ..."

"Who?"

"Yotta!"

"I don't know anybody named Yotta!"

And then the host hung up.

It was like a punch in the face. What an asshole, I thought.

"Come on, let's go to a club," I said to Maria, "we'll make our own party."

Ten minutes later we were standing at the door of a nightclub in Hollywood.

The security guy smiled at me and said: "ID, please!"

"ID? Huh? Do we look like we're eighteen?"

"No, but that's how it is in the US."

"I don't have my ID with me!"

"Then you're not coming in!"

Slaammm, the next punch to the face. *Welcome to Los Angeles!*

Twenty minutes later we were at home and I felt like a stinking dog that nobody wanted. What a start into our new lives and this new city. It wasn't how I'd imagined it.

Well-trained in positive thinking I immediately thought of the question:

What do I want instead? That was the magic question and I knew the answer immediately.

I was angry and said to Maria, full of energy, in fact, I shouted at her:

"Do you know what? Within a year everyone in this city is going to know me and will be standing at my door wanting to come in and not the other way around! Boom!"

I sent this vision into the universe. I saw it, I felt it, I believed in it. The universe was not able to resist all this bundled-up energy, and everything happened just the way I wanted. And even much better!

I became the Party King of L.A.

I threw parties like Hollywood had never seen before.

I had real lions at my parties, fireworks, live performances and of course the hottest girls, not just from the US but from around the world.

I rode a five-ton elephant through Hollywood to my own party, followed by seven police cars and a helicopter from a TV station. Eight hundred invited guests had the party of their life and about five hundred people stood outside, hoping to get in.

The *L.A. Times* wrote a three-paged article about me. I even made it on the front cover!

Six different TV stations camped out at my house.

I made it into newspapers in over fifty-two countries.

They called me the new Hugh Hefner and the Party King of Los Angeles.

And all that happened within a single year, just as I had proclaimed it would.

My vision had once again come true. I could have sunk my head that first day and thought that L.A. was probably just out of my league. But I got back up and took hold of my destiny with both hands.

Often the biggest successes arise from just such unfortunate situations. I am thinking about Mark Zuckerberg, who nobody wanted as a friend so he decided to start his own platform, where he could find online friends. The rest is history.

So whenever you go down on your knees – use the momentum to jump back up!

This reminds me of a conversation with a friend in Munich, which always makes me smile. He said to me: "Bastian, Hollywood is a totally different number, you can do what you want, no one's going to notice you!"

He was right, but only about our arrival on the first day. It's a good thing I didn't believe him.

And what only my guests know: at every party there were a ton of homeless people invited. I organized a gala for donations. I organized a job and an apartment for most of them and they are not on the streets anymore.

Party King or not, the streets had changed me and I became the good person that I always wanted to be. The media didn't take notice of this at all, a show-off sells better than a humanitarian champion. The masses prefer a more simple diet, which they can get excited about and the slaves to the media deliver.

It hurt me at first that the news reports about me were so extremely one-sided. By now I have risen above it. After three years, I'm pretty much over it – and working on the last two percent to change it to "completely over it."

The only thing that really matters is being true to yourself. Only you know who you really are. The others can only see you through their filter, and we know that only about two percent of this comes into consciousness and ninety-eight percent is blocked.

In summary:

1. Even when something starts horribly, you can turn your destiny around anytime.

2. Only go down on your knees to use the momentum to jump up again.

3. A failure often sets the best motivation in motion, so be thankful and take advantage of the opportunity.

4. Ask yourself what you want instead.

5. See it.

6. Feel it.

7. Believe in it.

It's always one and the same principle.

In my life money has played a major role, but it's about much more than just "money," so I'm going to explain to you how I envision the "Yotta Life."

The term itself means that you are trying to get to the highest level in your life. I'll leave it up to you how you want to define it, but *the sky is the limit* – and beyond!

*

There are five main areas in the Yotta Life in which I try to make progress every day.

1. Wealth

2. Health

3. Happiness

4. Love

5. Beauty

Every area actually deserves a book on its own, and perhaps I will write these five books. But first let's take a closer look at these areas in this chapter.

WEALTH – FOR THE LOVE OF MONEY

Money is the root of all evil, say those who don't have any.

I say: A lack of money is the root of all evil.

Because when people steal and do crooked things, it is usually because they have too little money.

To me, money is the most spiritual thing in the world.

This statement may provoke, but I'm happy to explain what I mean by that.

Money is a universal means of exchange. You can exchange it for almost anything that you want. What you exchange it for doesn't depend on the money but on your personality.

Luxury: you want the highlife – you need money.

Health: healthy food, alternative methods of healing, fine cuisine – you need money.

Knowledge: books, courses, cultural trips – you need money.

Family: children, school, university – you need money.

And the most important thing of all: Money can save lives. You support numerous charitable activities and change the lives of other people positively.

I always hear the statement: Money doesn't buy you happiness.

This stupid saying makes me want to puke – poverty definitely doesn't make you happy. Go to a kid in Africa who is suffering from hunger and tell him that money doesn't buy happiness.

I support a charity in Africa and I know what I'm talking about.

Money is neither good nor evil. Money exists. Period.

If you are an asshole without money, you will be a bigger asshole with money. If you're a good person without money, you'll be a very good person with money.

Money is like a magnifying glass, it enables you to act differently and reveals who you really are. What you do, depends on your character and not your bank account.

If you think money is bad, it will never come to you. Be a money magnet and a good person, then you can have a lot of fun in your life and also do a lot of good!

#2 HEALTH

I DON'T SMOKE.

I DON'T DRINK ALCOHOL.

I DON'T TAKE DRUGS.

I DON'T TAKE STEROIDS.

NEVER HAVE, NEVER WILL.

THAT'S RIGHT. NEVER. 0.0 PERCENT.

I PAY ATTENTION TO WHAT
I EAT AND EAT HEALTHY.

I DRINK A LOT OF WATER,
LOTS AND LOTS OF WATER.

I EXERCISE AND DO SPORT.

We only have this one body, so we should cherish and nourish it. That's exactly how a good German treats his car – and there are many other examples. But we are only given this one body, and we should keep it running at top level. This enables us to live and work with a very high energy level.

I want to point out that health includes mental health and so I also want to add that:

I DON'T WATCH TV.

I DON'T READ OR LISTEN TO THE NEWS.

I DON'T LISTEN TO MUSIC
WITH NEGATIVE LYRICS.

I READ A LOT.

I LISTEN TO MOTIVATING AUDIOBOOKS.

I SLEEP AT LEAST SIX HOURS A DAY.

I THINK POSITIVELY.

Keep your mind clean and don't fill it with garbage.

Try all of the above-mentioned behaviors for four weeks and then listen to your inner voice to see how you feel. If the difference is obvious, then I don't have to say another word.

It's up to you!

I am asked over and over again how I manage to function on such a high energy level without ever losing even a single percentage of momentum. Now you know how. And I have been writing this book for over seven hours now without a single break, and I'm still sitting here and feel fresh and full of energy.

Your energy will be boundless if you take loving care of your mind and body.

Success!

 **HAPPINESS**

The basis of our happiness is love – the love of ourselves.

Happiness is a feeling that only comes from within.

If you don't love yourself, you will have a hard time experiencing happiness. Usually feelings like envy and jealousy will take over.

There was a time when I couldn't love myself, because there were just too many things that I didn't like about myself.

But do you know what?

You can change everything!

Start analyzing your situation.

Write a list of all the things you don't like about yourself. Then take a second page and write the opposite of each of these points.

For example:

I am too fat. I am in shape und fit.

I don't finish things.

I persevere and finish what I start.

I don't know what I want. I know what I want.

Your list should be honest – don't gloss it over – because that's the only way you can find out how to get in harmony with yourself and fall in love with yourself again.

After the analysis you start the implementation.

- Get in shape.

- Do something to prove to yourself that you can follow through.

- Find out what you want.

- Create your own Hollywood movie, just as we've learned.

ANOTHER TOOL FOR HAPPINESS IS THANKFULNESS

However bad you're doing, there are always things that you can be thankful for.

Write down five things every day that you are thankful for.

Do it in the evening before you go to bed and in the morning before you get up.

It can be big things or little ones:

I am thankful, because ... I am alive.

I am thankful, because ... I can see, hear, taste and smell.

I am thankful, because ... I had such a great dinner, yesterday.

There are thousands of reasons to be thankful. Always use the words:

"I am thankful, because ..."

This is how you can invite happiness into your life. Try it!

MAKE SOMEONE HAPPY

If you make at least one person happy every day,
you will soon have a huge smile on your face.
This can also mean something little or big:

- Smile at a stranger or ask them
  how they are doing.

- Tell your mother, grandmother
  or sister that you love them!

- Give the cashier in the supermarket or
  the lady at reception, or anyone, who isn't
  expecting it, a little bouquet of flowers.

- Go into a nursing home and give
  someone, who doesn't have anyone,
  thirty minutes of your time.

- Say thanks to someone whose service you've
  always taken for granted. For example,
  walk up to an employee of the city parks
  and recreation department when you see
  them planting flowers and thank them for
  making the city so livable and nice-looking.

It is so great, believe me.

STOP WORRYING – TRUST AND ENJOY

Many people live in worry and fear. This is counter-productive to the law of attraction, because you will attract even more of what you are focused on.

Take advantage of the law of attraction. Visualize what you want. Feel it. Strengthen your belief with constant affirmations, trust in the law of attraction. Lean back until your wish is fulfilled, open your eyes and realize that you are in the here and now. Live and enjoy!

Life is happening right now. You can contemplate the future when it's there. Your wish has been sent off. The shipment will be delivered.

Don't worry, be happy! Says the famous song by Bobby McFerrin. I recommend that you listen to this song because the lyrics and the music will help you to feel it.

A quick guide to happiness:

1. Love yourself.

2. Be thankful every day.

3. Make one person a day happy.

4. Don't worry: trust and enjoy.

I could add another thirty points to this list, but the top four should be enough to get you started. You will soon begin to feel a big difference.

A quick reminder: You must live this book, not just read it, because it will change your life.

 #4 LOVE

I have written a lot about self-love, here are a few words about love itself.

One of my daily affirmations is:

I love the world and the world loves me.

I love life and life loves me.

And this is exactly what it's all about.

Your frequency should be tuned into love. That is the only emotion that can't be created artificially. Love is in the magic and allure of life. There is an infinite potential in you to love.

When you are operating on the frequency of love, magical things will begin taking place in your life.

I LOVE MYSELF.
I LOVE LIFE.
I LOVE THE WORLD.

These three sentences have a power that is far greater than you can imagine. Repeat these affirmations as long and as often as possible until they have become your permanent frequency. This is so easy, you only have to start.

Many haters immediately question how they can love the world when it is completely in chaos at the moment.

I answer with a smile:

In my two-percent perception of the world, it is good and beautiful because I believe in this.

If it isn't like this for you, then it is high time you change it.

The world is not what it is. The world is what we perceive it to be.

And of course there is war and suffering in the world, but you will not be able to change anything when you are sad and negative in your actions.

Love is the answer, sang John Lennon, and I join him in this knowledge.

You cannot change the world, but you can change the way you think. The more people do this, the stronger the influence of positive thinking on our world. We should begin immediately because that is something we can do.

So do it! Now!

I was not born beautiful, but I think I'm very beautiful.

Beauty is not a genetic characteristic.

Beauty is an attitude and a feeling.

Beauty means that you have made the best of yourself and feel good.

On the inside as well as the outside.

Beauty is in the eye of the beholder. What counts is that you think you're beautiful.

So do something about it. Take care of yourself. Indulge yourself with beauty for your body, mind and soul.

A new shirt, a good facial mask, a great book, a workout, a new haircut or just a lavish bath and a peeling. Whatever you need to feel beautiful, do it. Don't do it to please others. Do it for yourself.

It's about feeling good, because that is the frequency on which the universe transmits which influences the events in your life that are delivered to you.

Be beautiful. Be yourself.

I personally find a woman very attractive, when I sense that she finds herself attractive. That counts more to me than a few more pounds here or there. Confidence and charisma are sexy! That's why I use the term beauty for the body, mind and soul!

Find out how you define beauty and create the appropriate vision for yourself. I did that back when I was on the streets. I wanted to have a well-toned body and be really fit. I saw myself on Malibu beach with a six-pack. But I also wanted to have a beautiful soul and help other people. I created a concrete vision of a beautiful self. I saw this. I felt this. I believed in it. I became it.

Thinking that you are beautiful and loving yourself go hand in hand. Don't underestimate the importance of beauty.

MAKE THE BEST OF YOURSELF.
EACH OF US HAS THE POTENTIAL
TO BE A BEAUTIFUL PERSON.

Wealth, happiness, health, love, beauty.

Now you know the five pillars of the Yotta Life.

That is how I define Yotta Life and what I work towards every day. This is the work that is really important – your life is your currency.

That is what really counts. Balance the five pillars in your life so that they are in harmony.

Take part in life, feel alive and happy.

That is the work that is really important.

We will never achieve perfection, but we can become a little bit better every day.

Is that not what it's all about?

Is that not what we're living for?

YOU ARE
READING
THIS, SO YOU
ARE ALIVE.
THE BIG
QUESTION IS:

WHY?

6

THE MEANING OF LIFE – THE BIG WHY

Three years have gone by since I made California my home, and I still feel incredibly happy. I've become a star with my own TV show. I have made the name Yotta famous.

I have made a lot of things happen; building, redoing, undoing. It's unbelievable how much I've achieved.

An amazing journey. I have learned so much and experienced so much, I could write another five books about it. One thing always stays on my mind: I am still on this journey and always will be. Many of my fans write me: Yotta, you've made it!

What have I made?

I've made my Hollywood movie come true, that's right. And I achieved all that from the worst possible starting position of all. It's like the lyrics from the Bushido song: *From the curbside to the skyline*. I proved

that anything is possible. But do you know what? I already have a new dream, a new movie. It never stops. After the game is the same as before the game – says Sepp Herberger, the famous German soccer player and coach. After the dream is the same as before the dream, says Bastian Yotta. Up until the last second of my life there are two characteristics that I will always unite within me: I am thankful and I am hungry for more!

Imagine you are a soccer player and your dream is to play in the big leagues.

YOU ACHIEVE THIS GOAL.

THEN YOUR GOAL IS TO PLAY FOR YOUR COUNTRY IN THE WORLD CUP.

YOU ACHIEVE YOUR GOAL.

YOUR NEXT GOAL IS TO WIN AN INTERNATIONAL TITLE.

YOU ACHIEVE YOUR GOAL.

AND AFTER YOUR PLAYING CAREER YOU WANT TO BECOME A TRAINER TO PASS ON YOUR KNOW-HOW.

YOU ACHIEVE YOUR GOAL.

AND SO ON AND SO FORTH.

Whenever someone says you've made it on this journey, you would answer, yes, but I'm still hungry for more, even though I am thankful for everything that I've already achieved.

It is so much fun to let your dreams come true that I always set a new goal as soon as I've reached one. Because it is not only the goal which motivates me, it is the effect the goal has on me of allowing me to grow along the way towards achievement.

Shakespeare said: *The chase is more satisfying than the conquest.*

That doesn't sound that great to me, but at least I enjoy sowing the seeds as much as I do harvesting.

Is that what life is all about? Let's try with a bird's eye view and ask the question of all questions.

WHAT IS THE MEANING OF LIFE?

I have asked myself this question and have the answer, which I will share with you. However, first I asked myself another question, which also contains unbelievable power within:

WHAT DO I WANT TO THINK IN THE LAST SECOND BEFORE MY DEATH?

I will think: It wasn't all good, and it wasn't all bad. But it was my damn ride, without ifs or buts, and it was a cool ride! It was the real me, my way, my life!

Frank Sinatra hit the nail on the head when he sang: *I did it my way.*

This is what I want to think and what I'm going to think. I was me. I didn't pretend and I was true to myself. I have recreated myself over and over again. That's what it's about.

I hear again and again: Find yourself! That's nonsense.

Where should I look? I can only fall back on what's happened in the past, so the basis of my search would be limited to the past. That would be a very limited search. No thanks, I'll give it a pass. Life is unlimited!

I would use another word: instead of "find," use "invent" yourself.

Take this example: Many of you know my Superman Rolls Royce and my superhero costume. When I want to be Superman, I am Superman, and the next day I can be Batman or Mickey Mouse. I decide who I am.

That is the best gift life has to offer: our free will. We can think what we want. And as we have already learned: thoughts become a reality. So we can become who we always wanted to be.

Being a superhero is a feeling, that's all. Who you are is a feeling. It doesn't have anything to do with external factors. It doesn't have anything to do with your past. It's in your power to recognize that and take advantage of this new found wisdom.

I was a loser for long enough, a loser can't save the world. A loser only complains and blames others, and in this case life ends up being a one-way street.

A superhero can change things. He takes responsibility for his life and develops super powers, that he uses to make a difference. As we have learned, we all have super powers inside us, we just need to turn them loose.

Be a superhero! You can be whatever you want to be.

We need more superheroes and fewer losers.

You should live life. You should be happy and let your dreams comes true.

Don't dream away your life – live your dreams!

In the last second of my death I will definitely not think: "Oh well, if I had only ..."

No would have, could have, or should have!

Make sure that at the end of your life there are no "should haves" left.

This is why I love to create a bucket list of all the things that I still want to experience. At the end, every "should have" will have become an "I did."

Money, wealth, property are all transitory, but no one can take away your memories.

Collect some memories! We try to add more hours to our lives. I try to add more life to the hours!

There is only one catch. Nobody knows how much time they have left. The end can come tomorrow or in thirty years. We don't know.

So you should play it safe and start right now to transform "I would" and "I should" into "I did."

Is that the meaning of life?

Yes, that's about it, but there's still something else to add.

In order to understand the deeper meaning of life, we have to take a look at nature and the universe. A long time ago there was the proverbial big bang, and since then the universe has been continuously expanding. It has been growing for about thirty billion years, every single second it makes progress.

And it's the same with nature. It's growing every single moment.

Growth is what's all about!

We, as a part of this whole, as a part of the universe and nature, were created to do the same.

We must grow! We must make progress!

Children master this in an excellent way. We learn to grow up and make progress joyfully every day in countless different areas of life. As grown-ups, we stop doing this, our progress takes place in the hamster wheel of daily life. The term "grown-up" already sounds negative: We would never have to "grow up" if we lived in harmony with the universe!

The purpose of life consists of growing and making progress every single day. And now we've come to a very important point: The measuring stick for your growth is no other than you, yourself!

Your "me" of yesterday is your measuring stick for today. And your current version of today will be the measuring stick for tomorrow.

Never compare yourself with others. That doesn't make sense, it's about your life, and you are unique.

Life is progress. Life means being in motion, just like the universe.

When you stop moving, you're dead.

Unfortunately, there are many people who are alive, but not really living.

The time has come to give your life a purpose!

The time has come to figure out the big why – to know why you are jumping out of bed so early.

Many people think the big why is that you have to work and fulfill your obligations.

No, the big why is something else. Get up and give everything you have to be better than yesterday, to learn something, to make progress, have experiences, help others and be happy at the same time.

There is no way to happiness.

Happiness is the way!

Whether you dream of a life in Hollywood or a farm in Texas or the life of a millionaire or a monk – it doesn't matter. As long as it is your innermost dream, chase it and let it become a reality.

Go out and find your big why!

You are alive to awaken your dreams to life. Dream again. Dream loud and dream big.

I made it and you can too.

I have shared all my experiences with you and put the tools in your hands. Now go your own way. Every journey begins with the first step.

You bought this book and read it so you have already taken the first step. Congratulations!

Now it's time for the next step.

I will always be with you, at that moment when you don't know how to go on, just think: What would King Yotta do, and you will hear my voice.

Always remember: You are alive now. Your life is happening right now. Go out and make the best of it. We don't know how long we still have, it could all be over tomorrow. So use the time you have.

Your dream life is waiting for you. Go get it!

IF YOU WANT ANSWERS FROM LIFE, THEN ASK THE RIGHT QUESTIONS.

7

ONE MORE FOR THE ROAD ... - THE Q&A GAME

Those who have seen me on social media, know that I love the Q&A Game.

This chapter contains many helpful tips and words of wisdom. It is great for a quick check whenever you need some input. This helps to keep the book a part of your daily life.

It was my goal that you never read this book to the end, instead continue to open it up and discover something new.

This chapter will help with this. Read it and you will keep in the flow of the Yotta spirit and will reach your goal more quickly and easily.

I will simply ask a few questions on your behalf and then answer them. Every answer is meant to encourage you to become active yourself. The answers are *impacts*, like an engine being ignited. The motor is running but you've got to drive! Good luck with this explosive fuel!

NEVER SEARCH FOR THE RIGHT ANSWERS.
ASK THE RIGHT QUESTIONS!

Yotta, do you still have doubts and evil voices in your head, today?

Yes, every day I renew the fight against these voices. Every person has negative voices in their head. The question is whether you listen to them and let the negative soldiers in through the gate of your mind or not. Take advantage of what you have learned!

Yotta, what was your biggest mistake?

A mistake is something that you make over and over again, without learning from the negative consequences. I don't regret anything in my life because I learned from it. I have done a lot of things wrong, but through constant learning I have transformed the mistakes into something useful. I found many ways that don't work and that I don't have to try again in the future.

Yotta, what question should I ask?

As you can see from the example of my life story, I have asked myself the right questions over and over again. You must ask the right questions in life to get the right answers. Listen to your feelings. Listen to your inner voice. We're often too busy to hear it. But each of us has this voice, or rather: the instinct. I call it *living by instinct*. Our eyes, our ears, and our senses can be fooled. But not our feelings. Ask yourself the right questions and start your search for the answers.

Yotta, what is your biggest fear?

I have no fear, because fear is an illusion. You imagine that something bad can happen. Because I create the future with my thoughts, I don't devote my attention to fear, I can think about bad things, when they happen, but not before. When fears try to enter into my castle, I say "Stop!" and ask myself the magic question: What do I want instead?

Yotta, what is your biggest dream?

My dream is to be an international superstar, who inspires and motivates millions of people. At the same time, I want to save the lives of millions of people with my charity and enjoy my life to the fullest with my last and perfect partner, full of happiness, health, love and passion.

Yotta, is everything in your life without limits?

Very much, yes, but time is not, and so it's my most valued asset. I appreciate every day that I am given, and I make the most of it. Defend this asset from time wasters like social media or blithering idiots. Everything that has no benefit to your or doesn't create happiness is a time waster.

Yotta, what do you think about the setbacks in the past?

It was all an investment, to become better and stronger. Setbacks and challenges are the gym for your character and soul.

Make the most out of these moments for your personal growth!

Yotta, what mistake keeps most people from achieving success?

There are two, on the whole:

1. They don't control their thoughts and feelings and, therefore, what happens to them. Pay attention to your language, because it reflects what you are thinking. Thoughts become words. Words become actions. Actions become habits. Habits build your character. Your character determines your life. Always pay attention to what you think.

2. People are inactive. They know a lot, but that's worthless without the right action!

Yotta, how can I become rich?

Add value. Solve a problem for millions or worth millions.

It's all about your worth. The value of a sports team determines whether you play or not, the value of your company determines your income. And much more important: Develop your own worth, because self-esteem is the most important currency in life! You aren't rich unless you live life richly.

Yotta, how do you deal with haters?

The question should really be, how do the haters deal with themselves? I personally don't know hate and always try to feel love. Hate is an absolutely pointless waste of energy, which only attracts more hatefulness into your life. For this reason, haters are really only doing damage to themselves. If you are happy, you don't have room for hate. Let the haters hate and concentrate on being happy.

If your doorbell rings and the postman tries to deliver a package of hate to you, simply refuse the delivery. No thanks, bye-bye!

Many accept the hate, take it personally and don't understand how it could have come about. For the "why," there are many reasons, but the haters usually can't explain it to themselves. I do this affirmation every day: "I attract only positive people into my life," and it works.

Yotta, how should I handle negativity in general?

Don't ignore it, try to deal with it. Negativity is like an ocean on which your ship is sailing. As long as the water doesn't come into the ship, the ship will glide over the water and reach the harbor safely. Don't let the negativity come into you, glide over it. Refuse to give negativity any space in your thoughts. When it pops up, ask yourself immediately: What do you want instead?

Yotta, how important are goals in life?

Goals are the elixir of life. But much more important than the goal is how the goal changes you. That's why you should set goals that will allow you to grow and make progress. This is why I love the statement: "The journey is the reward and every step makes me stronger and better!"

Yotta, what criteria would you use to pick an employer?

Basically, I don't want to work to make others rich. I work to make progress. That's why it doesn't matter what the job pays. Ask yourself, how the job will change you. It's about personal development. All work is an investment in yourself.

Yotta, how do you treat your father now?

I never had the kind of father that I would have liked to have, but I had something grander than that. I had a Grand-Father. And I am infinitely grateful for that. I have forgiven my progenitor, and I am thankful for every lesson that I learned. Should he have to leave this world one day, I will be there for my mother and take care of her, if she wants that. I advise anyone with a similar fate: forgive, learn from your experiences and then close that chapter.

Yotta, what are the enemies of success?

There are too many to count – I could fill another book with them all. The worst enemies, however, are the ones that we don't recognize as our enemy. Such as the good friend who advises us to keep our feet on the ground so that we don't get disappointed when our dreams don't come true. Be cautious of your friends, they can be your biggest enemies without wanting to be!

Yotta, when is the best moment to make a change?

Not someday, but on day one: today!

If you don't begin something you want by taking the first step within twenty-four hours, then you will never do it ninety percent of the time. So come on, my friend, the clock is ticking!

Yotta, what can I do, I have so many problems?

Be bigger than your problems. If you do the same things this year that you did last year, you will have the same results again. So analyze your situation, then change it and then your life will change. I did and so can you.

Yotta, how come so many people fail even though they actually do know better?

Good question. The answer has to do with a time delay. We all start a project full of motivation and believe we are doing everything right, but then nothing happens. Then we get demotivated and impatient and start doing less and in the end we give up entirely.

Everyone knows the phenomenon of the gym visits at the beginning of the year. The gym is full, everyone has lots of New Year's resolutions. But after a month there are far fewer gym-goers and after four months only the hard core is left. My tip is: keep on going. Perseverance and discipline are necessary if you want to be successful.

Yotta, I don't know what I want!

Life is a buffet and sometimes we are overwhelmed and don't know what we should try. You know what? Just try things out at the buffet of life. Try going a few different directions, and if that wasn't it, change it. Be brave and above all *active* in discovering your true desires.

Yotta, my life is like a rollercoaster, what should I do?

Listen to Frank Sinatra's "*That's life*" and *enjoy the ride*. Don't think anymore about the rollercoaster, your affirmation should from now on be: "My life is stable and balanced!" It's so easy. Everything is possible. You are the master of your life, nothing is futile!

Yotta, what is your favorite quote?

If you think you can do it or you think you can't, you're right.

Yotta, who is your role model?

Arnold Schwarzenegger is a big role model, but so was my grandfather. Every person that you meet in your life can be a role model. We can learn something from a lot of people. A role model doesn't have to be for everything, you can have different ones for different areas of your life. So keep your eyes open, the next role model might come into your life today!

Yotta, what should I do when I'm finished reading the book?

Three things:

1. Read it again.

2. Act on what you have learned.

3. Recommend this book to someone who needs it.

Often we see more after taking a second look. Make sure that you have not missed something very important in the first reading.

Success is spelled DO. Act on your knowledge.

Help others. Give them this book or recommend this book. The more people who become happy, the better the world will be in which we all live.

With this in mind, I wish you from the bottom of my heart that your life is absolutely the greatest thing that could ever happen to you and that you wake up in the morning with a smile on your face and go to sleep with a smile in the evening.

Life is your own personal concert, you now know how to play.

Get started now ... Magical moments and true miracles are waiting for you.

In love and unity,

Yours, Bastian Yotta

Follow me on Instagram @yotta_life and @yotta_ coaching

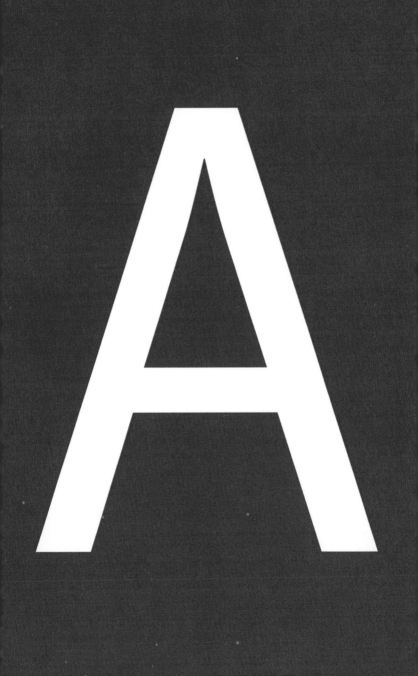

CKNOWLEDGMENTS

THANKS TO:

My Opa and my Oma – you were there for me. Your love and care were infinite and every memory is an unbelievable treasure in my life. I miss you and I will keep missing you until the day when we are reunited. I love you!

All my fans and followers, who send me countless messages of love every day and motivate me to inspire and give more.

My friend Wolfram, who has always been there for me and always manages to tell it like it is without me taking it personally. I am very happy to have you, my friend!

My bro Jad, who lit the spark that made me write this book.

My best friend Natalia, who supplies me with lunch and dinner, without whom I'd have forgotten to eat while I was writing this book, and I am sharing so many incredible fun and lovely moments with. And also big thank you for creating this amazing design for this book.

My buddy Mario, whose advice is filled with lots of energy and awareness and who read through this book with eagle eyes.

My great friend Liz, who never lets me down and is always there for me.

My beloved dog Luna, who has accompanied me for eighteen years through thick and thin and gives me so much love.

Myself: Thanks Bastian, that you didn't give up back then.

I thank all the people that I have encountered in my life. I was able to learn something from all of you and without other people it would be a damned lonely place on this planet.

So let's live together with our life's goal to respect the lives of others and our planet, and to love and make it better!

MY LOVE - LUNA. THE ONE WHO LOVED ME NO MATTER WHAT.

OU WANT MORE?
YOU'VE GOT MORE!

My online coaching continues on where this book leaves off ...

Get yourself a voucher with a value of twenty-five euros for your online coaching session on the topic of

- Money

- Body

- SuperMe

Voucher Code: YottaBible23

Redeemable at *www.yotta.university*

*

_____

*

The Deutsche Nationalbibliothek
Lists this publication in the Deutsche Nationalbibliographie; detailed bibliographic information
is available online at **http://d-nb.de**.

For questions and suggestions:
info@finanzbuchverlag.de

1st edition 2018

© 2018 by FinanzBuch Verlag, an imprint of the Münchner Verlagsgruppe GmbH,
Nymphenburger Straße 86
D-80636 München
Tel.: +4989 651285-0
Fax: +4989 652096

Translating: Shelley Steinhorst
Editing: Matthias Teiting
Proofreading: Hella Neukötter
Jacket design: Natalia Silva
Composition: inpunkt[w]o, Haiger (www.inpunktwo.de)
Printed in Germany

ISBN Print 978-3-95972-167-7
ISBN E-Book (PDF) 978-3-96092-307-7
ISBN E-Book (EPUB) 978-3-96092-306-0

Further informations are available at

www.finanzbuchverlag.de

Please notice our further imprints under www.m-vg.de as well.